Hydroponics for Everyone

In recent years millions of gardeners have taken up hydroponic or soil-less gardening following a world trend which was popularised by the astronauts. Plants are grown in cheap artificial soil and fed a mixture of water and minerals. The result is a non-stop supply of household vegetables, herbs and flowers. No digging or weeding needed!

This book describes how a lazy or even hopeless gardener can become a green-fingered horticultural wizard.

First published in 1986, *Hydroponics for Everyone* has proven one of the most popular books on the subject in Australia and overseas. Over 55 000 copies have been sold in Australia alone.

It has now undergone a major revision which brings together all the exciting new developments in hydroponics and new information on hydroponics societies and suppliers, etc. A further ten years of home hydroponicing has allowed the author to expand the range of practical advice. Queries and feedback from readers have been particularly useful in keeping the book as practical as possible. To make the book more helpful to readers in countries other than Australia and New Zealand, most measurements have been given in metric and in imperial units. No attempt has been made to convert Australian prices into other currencies. The prices stated are, of course, only a rough guide.

This is not a textbook for the potential commercial grower. It is designed so average gardeners can have a lot of fun and be rewarded for their efforts.

By S. K. Sutherland:

*Family Guide to Dangerous Animals and
    Plants of Australia*
Venomous Creatures of Australia
*Australian Animal Toxins: The creatures, their
    toxins and care of the poisoned patient*
Take care! Poisonous Australian Animals

Hydroponics for Everyone

A practical guide to gardening in the 21st century

Struan K. Sutherland
M.D., D.Sc., F.R.C.P.A., F.R.A.C.P.

Jennifer F.I. Sutherland
Dip. T., B. Theol., M.A. (Melb.)

HYLAND HOUSE

Dedication

To Anne Godden and Al Knight in appreciation of wise counsel and gentle encouragement.

First Published in 1986 by
Hyland House Publishing Pty Limited
Hyland House
387–389 Clarendon Street
South Melbourne
Victoria 3205 Australia

New edition 1987
Reprinted 1987, 1989, 1990, 1992, 1993, 1995
Revised edition 1996
© Struan K. Sutherland 1986 and Jennifer F. I. Sutherland
and Struan K. Sutherland 1996

National Library of Australia
Cataloguing-in-publication data:

  Sutherland, Struan K. (Struan Keith), 1936–
    Hydroponics for everyone: a practical guide to
    gardening in the 21st century

    Updated ed.
    Bibliography.
    Includes index.
    ISBN 1 875657 39 8

    1. Gardening — Australia. 2. Hydroponics —
    Australia. I. Sutherland, J. F. I. (Jennifer Frances
    Inglis), 1961–. II. Title.

  631.5850994

Photographs by the authors except where stated otherwise
Cartoons by Alison Sutherland
Designed and Typeset by Rob Cowpe Creative
Produced by Island Graphics Pty Ltd
Printed in Hong Kong

Acknowledgments

Many members of the Hydroponic Society of Victoria, especially their late President, Mr Phil Crespin, provided stimulating encouragement to write this little book. Dr Brian Hanger kindly gave permission to update an earlier survey he made of hydroponic suppliers in Australia. Mr Fred Funnell graciously checked the near final manuscript and suggested valuable improvements in the light of his experiences as both a teacher of and a practitioner of hydroponics.

My editor Anne Godden was the driving force behind both the original edition and the major revision of 1996. Anne contributed an exceptional amount of time, thought and effort. As the revision progressed so did the input by Jenny Sutherland increase to such an extent it was appropriate that she become a co-author. Apart from her precision typing, the useful suggestions made and practical help in setting up of subjects for photography, etc., has greatly enhanced the final result. However, where 'I' is used it usually refers to the more senior author. The only down side was that Anne had to deal with two authors instead of one!

We would like to thank our family and friends, whose voracious appetite for fresh hydroponic fruit and vegetables has almost exceeded production but certainly prevented any waste. As a good cook likes to see plates wiped clean so does the hydroponicer appreciate appreciation. Only weeds, snails and the local greengrocer disapprove of hydroponics as a hobby.

Contents

Confessions of a despairing gardener and how a dentist stopped the heartbreak

For twenty years as soon as the almond blossom had fallen and the frosts gone, this gardener went forth to plant his crops. Shirt off, he dug away and the smell of good earth rich with fat worms gladdened his heart. By dusk, guided by the accumulated wisdom of seed-packet journalists and years of television gardening hints on Friday nights, the mini paddocks were crossed with neat rows of seeds and seedlings.

A splendid sight this when the task is done. A reflective glass of chilled white wine is sipped and the lines of tombs from which will spring the family's peas and beans are slowly scanned.

One metre stakes tower over the starters in the annual Tomato Race — the gardener's equivalent to the Melbourne Cup — to have tomatoes ripe by Christmas.

Thus the stage is set. A few dollars worth of the nurseryman's best products are correctly planted and away we go. But do we? Technically I guess we do; however, if one analyses the events over the months leading up to summer's full heat, a rather sorry tale emerges.

First, the local cats consider freshly dug soil to be another indication of man's thoughtfulness. They are, however, a minor problem and probably only offend the gardener who rejoices in intact lines of greenery.

Second, most seedlings just sit silently meditating for months without any apparent desire to grow skyward. If and when they do take off, it's usually midsummer when they are positively geriatric. When at last harvest time comes the shops are inevitably overflowing with similar vegetables at rock-bottom prices.

Third, many seeds never seem to come up — if they do, they may just have a look around and die because of dryness at that critical time. A burst of heat in the middle of a working week is a common way young seedlings are lost or, conversely, a thunderstorm can sweep the lot down the nearest drain.

Fourth — weeds. These always appear to grow with great enthusiasm when the real crop is near static. Unless one is a retired person who inspects the garden daily, literally waiting for a weed to show its head — then in no time all is overrun.

Weeds seem especially designed to tangle their roots around individual seedlings so they participate unwittingly in a suicide pact when spotted by the enraged gardener.

And what a challenging variety of weeds there are: fern-like ones which cover everything and creeping brutes with deep roots which are easily left behind to sprout again a few days later. Weeds are very cunning. Specially so are the ones that seem to mimic the plant they are quietly suffocating.

Fifth — pests. Unwittingly most gardeners plant vegetables to feed pests. Earwigs apparently are the dedicated parents of the insect world but they have the charming nocturnal habit of making windows in new foliage. Stealthy cutworms emerge from the earth in the dead of night and devour young plants right down to ground level. All these assaults lead to more blanks in the row of seedlings.

Just by looking at the range of insecticides and fungicides on sale you will realise that the goal of natural home-grown vegetables is not easy to achieve.

Finally — watering and feeding. Unless this is regular and compatible with the growing plants'

needs, then stunted, diseased or even dead plants are the rule. The end product is often coarse or even woody as it reflects a stop – start growing cycle. When water restrictions are in force the chances of success are further diminished.

The above experiences are surely familiar to many a suburban gardener. Until 1980 I was resigned to repeating these cyclic experiences — each year commencing with enthusiasm but more and more inclined to limit my crops, say, to tomatoes and sweet corn which could rise above the weeds — or at least hide them.

Introducing Hydroponics

My introduction to hydroponics was quite accidental — but any frustrated gardener should be warned that once even a sniff of the sublime scent is inhaled, he or she may be hooked.

In 1980 I was having a one-way conversation with my elderly and distinguished dentist. He roams over a variety of subjects and the patient learns to emit gargling grunts of approval if a particular topic is of special interest.

Since he is fairly deaf one must make an appropriate, pithy and loud comment in the microsecond between spitting into the bowl and resuming the head back and mouth open position.

On this occasion the horticultural section of his discourse came earlier than usual. He had been relating his latest contact with a mutual friend —

a young scientist with whom he shares an interest in very superior photography.

He said, 'You should see Gordon's latest fad. He's into hydroponics. Do you know about hydroponics? (*Gurgle*) Growing plants without soil. He's got a little pump and tubes running around from a tank in his glasshouse. Tomatoes as big as baseballs — and at this time of year.'

'Beautiful lettuces growing in rows. It's fascinating. I thought, how can he find time to do this with his big garden and all his other interests? He says it's simple. Just takes a few minutes work every fortnight.

'The amazing thing is that when he picks a lettuce he just bungs a seedling back in its place and away it goes. You must talk to him about it. Did that hurt? Have a spit. Now open wider.'

In fact, I did talk to Gordon and his eyes shone with the gleam of a skier hearing a favourable snow report.

'It's wonderfully simple,' he explained. 'As a beginner you just need containers filled with an inert material to support the root system — sand or scoria is okay but you're better with a perlite and vermiculite mixture.

'It's a very light mixture and quite cheap and you can put it on the garden when you've finished with it. Put your plants in — make sure they are young ones and not those bonsai-like jobs that have sat around in nurseries for months.

'Add a bit of soluble complete plant food to your watering can and you're into hydroponics. In very hot weather you should water more often and make the solution a bit weaker. I'll give you some notes about it.'

Away I went. Over the next six months the family observed strawberries growing in profusion — no weed problems — and they grew so fast they had to be picked each night. Tomatoes were ready before Christmas and the second crop was still being picked in June. Chives grew like rice — tender clusters of green reaching 16 cm (6 1/3 in) high in six weeks.

I discovered some wonderful things about hydroponics. My plants seldom died prematurely, they grew rapidly and weeds were practically non-existent. Because the plants were healthy and vigorous, little if any pest control was required. If a grub did take up residence, it could usually be spotted a mile away by the damaged foliage. The rare hydroponic grub seems particularly plump when squashed! Another unexpected bonus was the ease of harvesting the crops since they are grown some height above ground level.

Inevitably, the next stage was for me to expand to a system which used a corrosion-resistant submersible electric pump to circulate the nutrient solution. I built a real Heath Robinson affair, with assorted hoses, drums, troughs and plastic bags. It leaked all over the place, looked absolutely dreadful, but worked. Now when I was at work on a boiling summer's day I could relax in the near certain knowledge that my pet plants at home had plenty to drink. The growth of plants improved even further and the family's routine vegetable needs were more than adequately met by hydroponics.

My next step was to make more use of the fittings available to the commercial hydroponic farmer. These allow leak-proof flexibility and are aesthetically quite pleasing. Tanks, tubing, elbow bends and cute little drippers are all black as the nutrient fluid is best protected from light to reduce the growth of algae.

Visitors found themselves on a compulsory hydroponic tour before aperitifs and there was no doubt that most lingered in an almost pensive fashion. Experienced gardeners confessed to latent hydroponic desires, whilst vegetarians salivated at the thought of masticating fresh insecticide-free foliage. Lovers of flowers stood reverently beside giant carnations which would often last a fortnight when picked. All in all, most people wanted to try their own hands at the art but many found various barriers in their way.

This book aims to make hydroponics accessible to gardeners everywhere and to offer a choice of options to suit each individual.

Struan K. Sutherland

Oh, Adam was a gardener, and God who made him sees
That half a proper gardener's work is done upon his knees.
    'The Glory of the Garden'
    Rudyard Kipling, 1865–1936

When you grow by hydroponics —
No stress on joints, no need for tonics.
so leave the weeds to poor old Adam
And come and try this brand new fadam.

Know what you're doin'
By gardening with Struan.

Save many a penny
By following young Jenny!

Preface

In recent years millions of gardeners have taken up hydroponic or soil-less gardening following a world trend which was popularised by the astronauts. Plants are grown in cheap artificial soil and fed a mixture of water and minerals. The result is a non-stop supply of household vegetables, herbs and flowers. No digging or weeding needed!

This book describes how a lazy or even hopeless gardener can become a green-fingered horticultural wizard.

Now that you have read this far it is fair to tell you that sloppy or hopeless people will be as useless at hydroponics as they are at everything else.

However, if for once in their lives these people decide to try to do something properly, then hydroponics could be an ideal activity. Plants are clever and may well provide early encouragement which can lead to confident participation in a rewarding hobby.

Undoubtedly, an interest in or understanding of hydroponics will markedly improve the results of conventional gardening.

There are many reasons why people become enthusiastic about hydroponics. Our personal ones are that results get better and more exciting all the time. Many opportunities constantly emerge to try new plants and to improve upon methods. Globally, the use of hydroponics has become an integral part of horticulture in many countries. This phenomenal expansion of commercial hydroponics

Commercial production of cucumbers by Bruce Laffer near Hobart, Tasmania. Panda film gullies sit on metal trays. An excellent example of the successful use of the nutrient film technique, see Chapter 4. (*Courtesy Roger Fox*, Practical Hydroponics and Greenhouses)

<u>Above</u>: Large-scale raising of plants in polystyrene trays with expanded clay as the medium, at the Fensmore operation at Kellyville in outer Sydney, New South Wales. Fensmore successfully market huge numbers of hydroponic indoor plants, using the Swiss-developed Luwasa system. This makes use of specially designed pots with an inbuilt water-level indicator which tells at a glance when topping up is required.
(*Courtesy Roger Fox*, Practical Hydroponics and Greenhouses)

<u>Right</u>: Commercial production of herbs at Classic Herbs, using flood and drain tables, see pages 38 and 39. (*Courtesy Roger Fox*, Practical Hydroponics and Greenhouses)

Kelly and Jane eating hydroponic tomatoes.

is due to a number of rational economic factors. The photographs show some of the developments in commercial hydroponics in Australia.

Through hydroponics many arid areas can maximise the use of precious water. In overcrowded regions the compactness of hydroponic systems, e.g. they can be placed on rooftops, has obvious advantages. The energy crisis has increased the cost of fertilisers and pesticides and to use these more effectively through hydroponics is a sound practice. In many parts of the world labour costs and availability of labour make efficient hydroponics an attractive proposition. From the consumers' view hydroponic produce is generally of superior quality and successive crops make the items available over a longer period.

Apart from economic advantages, there are environmental benefits to the use of hydroponics and environmental issues are having an increased impact on horticultural practices everywhere. The pollution of many streams and water tables by run-off from fertilisers and pesticides has become excessive and so the more efficient use of nutrients, especially their recycling, and later safe disposal, has advantages for everyone.

Measures to reduce pollution by nutrients are being enforced, for example, in Holland. This country has some 10 000 hectares (24 700 acres) of glasshouses and the seepage of nutrients and fertilisers into the water table is reaching a crisis level. With hydroponics the human can be in complete control and effective barriers between outlets to the land and the recycled hydroponic nutrients should almost eliminate this problem.

Furthermore, in hydroponics the use of sprays to deal with insect pests and diseases can be dramatically reduced by strict hygiene procedures and quarantining the hydroponics unit. Many commercial hydroponic establishments will not allow anyone other than their specially trained staff into their greenhouses. And, as we shall see, even amateurs will get better results if they follow some of these practices.

Few hobbies offer greater opportunities for inventiveness. Every established homemade hydroponic system is unique in the combinations of plants, containers and media used. Again and again I have seen someone starting off hesitantly with a few hydroponic plants and in no time at all they are in full swing and showing off rows of beautiful plants growing in a system made from local 'bits and pieces'.

In life we all dabble in things, one day showing great enthusiasm for a hobby then dropping it the next. The hobby of hydroponics has stayed with me because it is fun and, now that the unit is running effectively, it is no big deal. To be frank, there is also the reliability factor. There is no way I would go back to, for example, growing tomatoes out in the garden. Our household and the neighbours have been utterly spoilt and now largely rely upon hydroponics, especially for summer salads.

A number of amateurs have gone on to establish successful commercial hydroponic enterprises. They are the exception, as there are many pitfalls which await the unwary. To succeed in such an endeavour one must have a business plan which has passed the most rigorous examination as well as ongoing access to the best horticultural advice available.

A cautious approach should be adopted towards investment in any hydroponic development. They are no different from any other investments and will range from the shonky to ones well worth considering. Some enterprises may even be illegal with the final product intentionally going up in flames. Such ventures are often discovered when some fitting breaks loose and the apartment below the hydroponic unit is flooded. The situation can get quite messy — what with the police taking one line of action and the landlord and tenants facing the problems of water damage!

Finally, gardening is probably the commonest leisure time activity after watching television. Hydroponic gardening can be more rewarding than conventional gardening and, for the elderly or handicapped person, an appropriate hydroponic system can make gardening as easy as for anyone else.

A Brief History of Hydroponics

The modern science of hydroponics really took off about 1936 when the experiments of Dr W. E. Gericke at the University of California attracted a great deal of publicity. He grew a wide range of crops hydroponically, including tomatoes which grew to a height of 7.5 metres (24 ft 7 in) in twelve months. Gericke publicised the commercial potential of hydroponics and coined its name from the Greek *hudor* for water and *ponos* meaning labour. Thus hydroponics means literally working with water. We shall return to Gericke shortly.

From early times people have practised the growing of plants without soil. The famous terraced or hanging gardens of Babylon were partially hydroponic. Floating gardens in China were described by Marco Polo and both the Aztec civilisation and ancient Egyptians practised forms of hydroponics. About the time that the Spanish Conquistadors were wiping out the Aztecs, and presumably their gardens, in the sixteenth century, the first scientific studies on plant growth were taking place in Europe. The Belgian van Helmont carried out a delightfully simple experiment to show that the bulk of the weight of a plant does not come from the soil. He filled a drum with 200 pounds of dried soil, planted a 5 pound willow shoot and for five years watered it with rainwater. At the end of this period the willow weighed 160 pounds but the soil had lost only 2 ounces in weight. He concluded correctly that much of the

DR GERICKE'S
7·5 METRE
TOMATO PLANT
(1936)

weight gain. Furthermore, growth was impossible without absorption by the roots of nitrates and other minerals.

Over the next few decades chemists analysed the elemental composition of plants and were able to improve the nutrient solutions in which they were experimentally grown. By 1938 Hoagland had perfected the formula of his solution, which remains one of the commonest still used today.

In about 1925 sections of the American greenhouse industry became interested in artificial nutrient solutions, oddly enough because of the advent of the motor car and a growing shortage in supplies of suitable horse manure. By 1931 the description of a method for raising greenhouse carnations using washed sand and soluble nutrients instead of soil was published. Meanwhile, Gericke had been concentrating on 'floating' plants over a well aerated, heated nutrient solution and this technique was very successful but was technically difficult. A simplified version of this method is described on pages 47–9. Gericke deserves the title of founder of modern hydroponics since the imaginations of both the lay and scientific communities were captured by the possibilities of his method and its results. However, large-scale applications

weight gain came from water, but failed to realise that carbon dioxide and oxygen were also required. One wonders what else van Helmont did over the five years as well as watering his willow tree.

In England in 1699 John Woodward grew plants in water to which he had added varying quantities of soil. He concluded that substances dissolved from the soil promoted growth and that the bulk of the soil itself was not necessary.

Priestley discovered in 1722 that green plants sealed for some time in a container rich in carbon dioxide produced oxygen. Within two years Jean Ingen-Housz had shown that strong sunlight accelerated the production of oxygen and that it came only from the green parts of the plant. In 1804 Nicholas de Saussure published proof that water and carbon were fixed in plants at the same time and resulted in

THE END OF AZTEC HYDROPONICS

Darling Mills, a city restaurant, grows its own fresh produce on a rooftop in the heart of Sydney.

A Shows nutrient film tables on a glass platform over the swimming pool.

B Lemon, anise, cinnamon and purple varieties of basil are grown.

C An overhead conveyor belt with its decorative pots of herbs adds an aesthetic touch.
(*Photos courtesy Roger Fox*, Practical Hydroponics and Greenhouses

were few until 1944 when the United States used hydroponics methods to grow vegetables for troops stationed on remote bases in the Pacific and elsewhere. It was proven that an installation covering one-quarter of a hectare (0.6 acre) could provide one large salad per day for four hundred men.

After the war the development of hydroponics proceeded slowly and steadily until the last decade when its growth has been positively explosive. There have been many reasons for this, the main one being that once someone has shown an application to be a commercial success others will take it up and a chain reaction develops. Increased commercial importance led to ancillary industries and better equipment. Research, both Government sponsored and private, expanded the hydroponic techniques available and more and more countries are finding that hydroponics allows them regularly to provide fresh foodstuffs which previously could only be imported at great expense.

Often persons not the slightest bit interested in gardening see something on television which drives home some spectacular if specialised aspect of hydroponics. Some of the best film footage has come from Japan. A scientific exhibition in Tsukuba, Japan, displayed a magnificent 14 metre (46 ft) high tomato plant which, in the seven months since it was seeded, bore more than twelve thousand luscious red tomatoes! The same exhibition displayed a cucumber 'tree' with over three thousand cool, crisp cucumbers dangling amongst its foliage.

In many supermarkets hydroponic tomatoes and/or lettuces are available as a routine. In colder places the early appearance of hydroponic tomatoes is welcomed by shoppers who buy them in preference to others. Even the smallest fruiterer acts as an outlet for hydroponic products, be they salad vegetables or herbs.

Hydroponics is here to stay and all the indications suggest that to date we have only seen a minute fraction of the role it will play in the 21st Century.

CHAPTER 1

How a Plant Works – Its Basic Requirements

This chapter is the most important in the whole book. It should be read regularly if you love your plants.

For a plant to be fast growing and productive, all its basic requirements must be satisfied. If any one of these is inadequate, the poor plant will struggle on sending out frantic messages to passing humans until it expires. The needs of plants are not really very different from those of the family cat. Let us compare them.

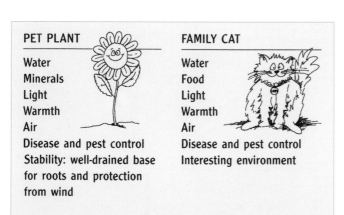

PET PLANT	FAMILY CAT
Water	Water
Minerals	Food
Light	Light
Warmth	Warmth
Air	Air
Disease and pest control	Disease and pest control
Stability: well-drained base for roots and protection from wind	Interesting environment

In other words, never put a plant in a situation that would eventually kill a cat or vice versa. Frankly, I think plants like an interesting environment as well — they certainly look better in one.

We have all studied plants at school but at that stage few kids have the slightest interest in gardening and, in fact, just wish things like lawns didn't grow so well. As we now want our plants to grow magnificently I would like to offer you a crash refresher course in plant function (see picture of the happy plant on page 2).

Let's start with the roots, which do a number of jobs. One is to hold the plant in the ground, and another is to send out little hairs to absorb water, minerals, carbon dioxide and oxygen. These fine hairs also excrete certain unwanted chemicals.

If the sun is shining when the sap reaches the green leaves, then energy is absorbed by chlorophyll in the leaves. This energy combines with the water (sap) and carbon dioxide from the air to make carbohydrates like glucose. The plant breathes out oxygen. This remarkable process is called 'photosynthesis' or making from light. When the sun sets, photosynthesis stops and, in fact, reverses. Some of the carbohydrate breaks down to release energy to build new cells to extend the roots and make new leaves and stems, etc. The plant now breathes out carbon dioxide. The small amount of soluble minerals taken up by the roots plays a vital part in all these events. Photosynthesis is one of Nature's greatest inventions and it is the same for a cabbage as a mighty river red gum. Without it mankind would be nearly extinct within months.

Here is a fact to recall next time you are admiring a giant river red gum. Of its total mass, 98 per cent comes from the combination of water and carbon dioxide, only 2 per cent is taken from the soil in minerals. When it is burnt the cycle reverses, the stored sun energy is released as heat, carbon dioxide and water return to the atmosphere and the minerals are left as ashes. I regularly drive past a fine old gum tree in Dendy Street, Brighton, and it

HYDROHINT
If a healthy young plant is not growing it's not its fault. Check the list under the pet plant.

constantly reminds me of the building power of photosynthesis as it ticks over quietly each day.

Now that we are experts on the inner secrets of plant growth, let's start again at the bottom and enlarge on some of the ingredients.

Water

This should be adequate otherwise the plant will spend most of its energy extending its roots to keep up with demand. Lack of water may lead to a huge and busy root system and a small miserable plant above the ground. On the other hand, the roots can literally drown if drainage is so poor no air can regularly get to the root hairs. The miles of tunnels around the roots made by the noble earthworm help keep the soil well ventilated and drained.

Plants use up a surprisingly large quantity of water. For example, a fast-growing tomato plant processes some 2.5 litres (0.66 US gal) per day and

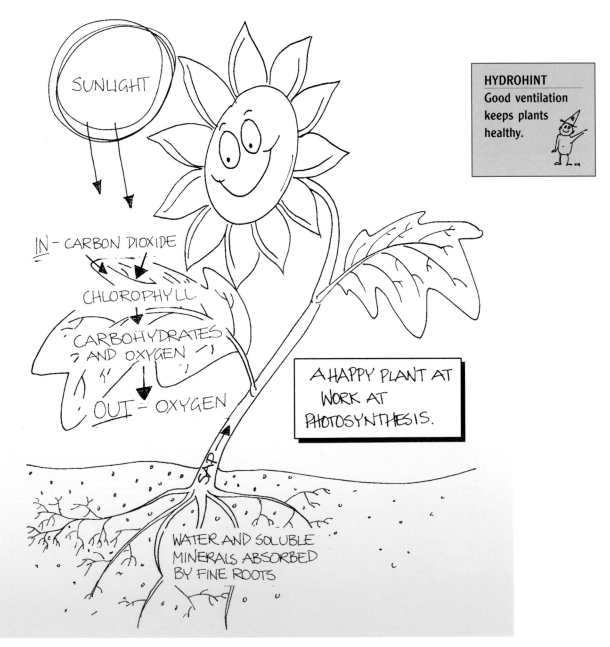

HYDROHINT
Good ventilation keeps plants healthy.

SUNLIGHT

IN - CARBON DIOXIDE

CHLOROPHYLL

CARBOHYDRATES AND OXYGEN

OUT - OXYGEN

A HAPPY PLANT AT WORK AT PHOTOSYNTHESIS.

SAP

WATER AND SOLUBLE MINERALS ABSORBED BY FINE ROOTS

A simple recycling system, see page 38, this salad box contains lettuce, radishes and spring onions.

A rare sight in Melbourne. A crop of tomatoes ready for harvesting in July.

A giant river red gum from the Barmah Forest, Victoria.

This wilting basil shows you what happens if you forget to water a plant!

Container with sweet William
and lobelia.

a fully grown strawberry plant requires at least 600 ml (0.16 US gal) per day.

Finally, the water should be as pure as possible. Toxic contaminants, such as a build-up of common salt, will stunt or kill most plants.

Hydroponics ensures a regular supply of uncontaminated water to the roots as well as adequate drainage.

Water-soluble Minerals

When keen gardeners put dried horse manure on their roses, the root system does not feed on bits of manure and send them up to the plant above. Bacteria and worms in the soil have first to break the manure down to release the minerals or nutrients. They can then be dissolved in water, taken up by the roots and ascend to the foliage.

Scientists over the years have worked out exactly which minerals are required in what quantities for most plants. Thus we see in our gardening shops an assortment of 'complete plant foods'. Nitrogen, phosphorus, calcium and potassium are the big four quantity wise and the other eight are sulphur, magnesium, iron, manganese, boron, zinc, copper and molybdenum. The last few are essential only in

minute quantities and hence their common name 'trace elements'. When good manure or a blood and bone mixture breaks down in the soil, all these minerals are released slowly and steadily. The suggested proportions of these minerals and the effects of a lack of them are discussed in the next chapter.

A well set up hydroponic system feeds the correct nutrient mixture directly to the roots and so we know the plant has access to sufficient food.

Warmth and Sunlight

Given adequate nutrition (water and soluble minerals) the plant now needs warmth and sunlight. If the ground is too cold, the root system will remain sluggish. We often see this in spring when the sun is pleasantly warm to the human but little heat penetrates into the soil. A few days of hotter weather and plant growth will dramatically increase. The best all-round temperature for most plants is about 22°C (72°F). Once the temperature falls below 15°C (59°F) or rises above 30°C (86°F), plant growth slows. The ideal amount of sunlight varies from plant to plant but for our purposes we will assume our healthy growing plants will happily accept as much sunlight as possible provided they

The perfection of a hydroponic rose.

are not being cooked. Some optimum root zone temperatures are given in Table 1.

In hydroponic gardening the unit can be moved about according to the season, or it can be placed in an established environment.

Table 1 SOME OPTIMUM ROOT ZONE TEMPERATURES			
Broad beans	25°C (77°F)	Strawberry	25°C(77°F)
Cucumber	29 (84)	Sweet corn	30 (86)
French beans	25 (77)	Tobacco	28 (82)
Peas	22 (72)	Tomato	27 (81)

Air

Plants require adequate air both above and below the ground. The oxygen around the roots is particularly important as it accelerates the plant's uptake of nutrients. A good hydroponic medium will ensure more oxygen is available to the roots than in even the best of soils. The roots will also have access to oxygen dissolved in regularly circulating nutrient solution.

Poor ventilation encourages the growth of mould and mildew and air movement can be improved by removing spent or excess foliage.

Hydroponic units are usually elevated off the ground, which promotes good plant ventilation.

Disease and Pest Control (see Chapter 8)

A healthy plant is less likely to be infected, eaten up or sucked dry by its many enemies. People who are opposed to using various garden sprays should keep their plants in top condition and promptly remove ageing or afflicted specimens.

Hydroponic plants are usually healthier than garden plants as it is easier to segregate them from potential enemies.

Shelter and Support

A plant buffeted by strong winds really finds it hard to concentrate on growing. Foliage is torn off, the stem is twisted and stressed one way and then the other, excess strain is placed on the root system, and the whole plant develops a miserable appearance. Thus, some degree of shelter is essential to most plants as is support to those which need it. Without support many plants cannot spread their foliage to take up as much sunlight as possible. They also breathe better and, being healthier, are more resistant to disease.

Hydroponic plants can be moved to shelter or grown in a protective environment. Supports can be attached to the plant containers or constructed around them.

How a Plant's Needs Are Satisfied by Hydroponics

Let us now transfer our happy plant (page 2) into a very simple hydroponic system. This will show how hydroponics is really just a method of improving the plant's support and feeding system.

Our plant is in a container (see the picture) and the earth has been replaced by a stable inert material called the *medium*. Many types of substances such as sand, scoria or perlite can be used as a medium and these are described in Chapter 3. The medium:

1 provides support for the root system;
2 retains some of the nutrient solution to be absorbed by the roots;
3 allows good drainage so the roots have adequate access to air;
4 provides some protection to the roots against extremes of temperature.

> **HYDROHINT**
> Drain your plant well. Poor drainage will result in a sick root system below and a miserable-looking plant above.

Fresh medium, unlike earth, has absolutely no nutritional value to the plant so nutrient is applied regularly in the form of a *nutrient solution* made up of the soluble minerals dissolved in good quality water. Some of the solution is poured into the container from a jug which is then positioned to

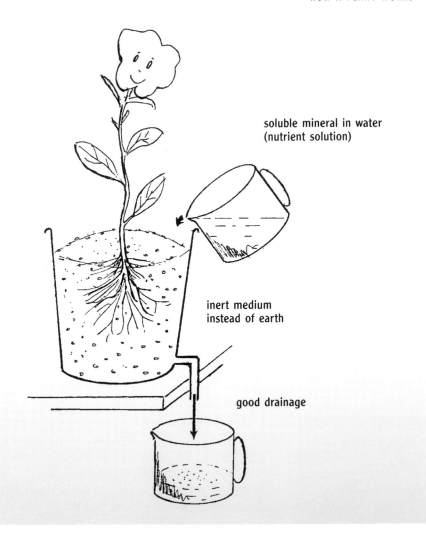

A very simple hydroponic system.

soluble mineral in water
(nutrient solution)

inert medium
instead of earth

good drainage

collect the solution as it drains out. In this way the medium is kept well stocked with both water and nutrients and the root system can help itself according to its needs.

The plant is free from soil and hence less likely to suffer from disease or pests. It stands alone and is not threatened by weeds or encroachment by other plants.

> Provided that the medium is suitable and the supply and composition of the nutrient solution is adequate, it should grow as well as, if not better than, earthbound contemporaries in similar conditions.

The sentence in the box should be re-read by anyone thinking of becoming physically involved with hydroponics.

Remember this quotation from William Bliss: 'Plants are very sophisticated and clever, they don't fight and they don't run across the road for a bone. Plants won't eat what they don't want to.'

HYDROHINTS
Avoid extremes of hot and cold. If conditions are uncomfortable to the hydroponicer, the plants won't be happy either. Try to maintain a balmy environment.

Plant Food and Nutrient Solutions

Some people find hydroponics discouraging when they read complex instructions about mixing twelve or thirteen different chemicals and then testing the concentration of the mixture and its degree of acidity or alkalinity. There are very few amateurs who mix their own chemicals; most of us rely upon the skills of the manufacturers who market premixed chemicals or minerals designed for hydroponics. As discussed later in this chapter, if we intelligently use a good mixture specifically designed for hydroponics then complex monitoring of the changes which may occur in the solution is unnecessary. Let us now look more closely at the essential minerals which were skimmed over in the last chapter.

Essential Minerals

The information contained in Table 2 is the result of years of research by many scientists. Although it looks complicated it is useful because it stresses the proven importance of the minerals listed. Deficiency states are far more common than toxic effects due to mineral excess. In fact a person would have to be extremely careless, especially in hydroponics, to produce a mineral overdose. A marked excess of any mineral usually causes severe burning followed by collapse and death of the plant.

A plant may, to a variable extent, develop deficiencies in a number of minerals. The overall appearance of the plant, therefore, may not be as much help to diagnosis as when a single 'classic' mineral deficiency occurs. The commonest deficiencies which occur in hydroponic systems are those of nitrogen, iron and magnesium.

Fed and starving plants: two French beans, both three weeks old, growing in vermiculite. The tall plant has received nutrient solution, the other only water.

Table 2 ESSENTIAL MINERALS, THEIR ROLE IN PLANT GROWTH AND SIGNS OF DEFICIENCY OR EXCESS

	SIGNS OF DEFICIENCY	SIGNS OF EXCESS (toxic effects)	
Nitrogen (nitrate and ammonium)	Plants spindly. Leaves small and yellowish. Parts of plant may turn purple. The new leaves of tomatoes point vertically. Older strawberry leaves may become red.	Plant too vigorous, becomes very leafy with dark green leaves, fruit ripening delayed. Susceptible to pests. Ammonium excess can cause root damage if bacteria are inadequate.	
Phosphorus	Plants are small and dark green. Lower leaves become yellow and may have purplish tinge as phosphorus is drawn from them to the new growth. Leaves curl backwards and droop. Fruiting is poor and root system reduced.	No direct toxicity. Reduced copper and zinc availability.	Phosphorus-deficient tomato. (*Courtesy Kevin Handreck*) 
Potassium	Plant growth slows, older leaves develop brown mottling. Flowers are fewer and plant is prone to fungus.	Uncommon to absorb a toxic amount. A secondary manganese deficiency may occur.	Potassium-deficient petunia. (*Courtesy Kevin Handreck*)
Calcium	Plant stunted with crinkled leaves. Youngest parts die and bloom falls. Calcium-deficient tomatoes may get brown spots on blossom end of fruit. These spots may decay (blossom rot) particularly with sudden onset of hot weather.	No specific changes.	
Sulphur	Uncommon. Young leaves become yellow with purple changes at leaf bases.	Slowed growth and small leaves.	Stocks showing sulphur deficiency. (*Courtesy Kevin Handreck*)
Iron	A common deficiency. New growth pales and blossom drop occurs. Yellowing initially seen between veins, and leaves may die from the edges. In tomatoes this deficiency may occur when fourth or fifth cluster is developing and nutrients are being diverted from rest of crop.	Very uncommon. Usually seen as black spots after spraying with nutrient.	 Iron-deficient grevillea. (*Courtesy Kevin Handreck*)

Table 2 CONTINUED

	SIGNS OF DEFICIENCY	SIGNS OF EXCESS (toxic effects)	
Magnesium	Older leaves curl and yellow areas appear between leaf veins. Only youngest leaves remain green. (A 'mobile element' which moves from older to newer leaves.)	Not described.	
Boron	Brittle stems and poor growth. Tomato stems may become twisted and sometimes split with the centre looking like cork.	Leaf tips become yellow and then die.	Manganese-deficient lettuce. (*Courtesy Kevin Handreck*)
Manganese	Yellowing of leaves between the veins and buds fail to bloom.	May reduce availability of iron.	
Zinc	Small leaves sometimes with crinkled margins.	May reduce availability of iron.	
Molybdenum	Leaves small and yellowish.	Rare. Tomato leaves may become bright yellow.	
Copper	Pale yellow-spotted leaves.	May reduce availability of iron.	Copper-deficient snapdragon. (*Courtesy Kevin Handreck*)

Deficiency states are easily avoided by following a routine schedule of feeding and not postponing preparation of a fresh batch of nutrient solution. Regular and adequate feeding, especially during periods of rapid growth, is as important to plants as it is to children.

The plant may continue to look fine while you are being forgetful or lazy but the results of this period of involuntary dieting will become evident a few weeks later.

A reliable supply of correctly balanced minerals will allow the plant to go merrily about its business of growing without suffering any of the dismal effects of starvation (see the photograph on page 8).

Ratio of Nutrients

Literally hundreds of hydroponic formulations have been invented over the last thirty or more years. Many of these are designed for specialist crops. Others just illustrate some of the millions of variations possible whilst including the range of nutrient concentrations shown in Table 3.

Suppliers of nutrients made for hydroponics use formulas near the average shown in the table. The regulations insist that an elemental analysis is included on the label and, as the number of manufacturers increases, one can be more selective, particularly when buying in quantity. Preference should be given to those which incorporate iron in the chelate form rather than in the less stable ferrous sulphate because a premature deficiency of iron is less likely to develop.

Variation in Ratio of Nutrients

Until recently, it was generally recommended that in winter the level of potassium be increased and nitrogen decreased. Some manufacturers produce separate summer and winter mixtures. This varia-

Table 3 CONCENTRATION OF NUTRIENT ELEMENTS IN HYDROPONIC SOLUTIONS IN PARTS PER MILLION (ppm)*

ELEMENT	LIMITS	AVERAGE USED
Nitrogen (nitrate form)	70–300	200
Nitrogen (ammonium form)	0–31	25
Phosphorus	30–90	40
Potassium	200–400	250
Calcium	150–400	160
Sulphur	60–330	70
Iron	0.5–5.0	4.0
Magnesium	25–75	50
Boron	0.1–1.0	0.2
Manganese	0.1–1.0	0.7
Zinc	0.02–0.2	0.05
Molybdenum	0.01–0.1	0.04
Copper	0.02–0.2	0.07

* i.e. milligrams per litre

HYDROHINT

Check that your nutrient powders dissolve up completely. If they don't, complain to the retailer or manufacturer.

---

tion is warranted in the long North American and European winters but does not appear necessary under temperate conditions.

On the other hand some commercial growers have specialised formulas not only for individual crops but also for the different stages of maturation of those crops. It's a matter of 'horses for courses'; for example, a commercial lettuce grower will use a solution with a proportionally higher nitrogen content than would be used by a tomato grower. Fortunately, however, most plants do perfectly well on a general purpose nutrient mixture.

To Buy or To Make Up One's Mineral Mixtures?

The chemicals used in a nutrient mix don't come in containers labelled 'nitrogen' or 'potassium' but as chemical compounds which often deteriorate in time or react adversely with each other if incorrectly mixed.

For most people, it is time consuming and a false economy to purchase some thirteen chemicals and then proceed with weighing and mixing. It is far better to calculate the minimum amount of nutrient mix required and then shop around for the best bargain. Buying in

HYDROHINT
Use only the best nutrient mixtures.

bulk often reduces the price most significantly, and you may find that your local hydroponics society bulk-buys from a reputable manufacturer. Starting off with a product that is known to work increases the chances of success from the word go.

Most commercial preparations are hygroscopic, that is, they absorb moisture. To avoid the mixture setting like a soft concrete, the containers should be kept well sealed. If you have a large drum of nutrient, its contents will probably be kept in good condition for months if you transfer some nutrient to a smaller container and use this material for topping up your hydroponic system. This will markedly reduce the chances of moisture getting to the bulk material.

If readers wish to mix their own minerals, they should consult the books listed in the Bibliography. Other hydroponic writers have no inhibitions about providing recipes for mixtures. Personally, I cannot think of anything less likely to enthuse one's household towards hydroponics than filling up the kitchen or laundry with bags and bottles of chemicals. Far better is a neat little drum of premixed nutrients.

When beginners have gained some experience they may decide to make up their own mixture. In correspondence, Mr Bill Meehan, former president of the Cairns Hydroponics Society, made the highly valid point that if any signs of deficiency should develop the extra minerals required are then on hand. This is particularly useful in the tropics where additional calcium and iron are often needed. Respected opinions like Bill's made me reconsider including a recipe for mineral mixes. However, the more I looked at the recipes the stronger became my original feeling that it was in the beginners' best interests to steer them away from making up their own mixtures. I hope Bill appreciates my motives.

The discerning reader may conclude that I have no experience in making up such mixtures. Years ago, for a research project on poisonous octopuses,

I had to prepare artificial seawater using umpteen chemicals. Octopuses sometimes died as a result of a technician making a slight mistake in calculations or the weighing out of a chemical. This experience has biased me towards taking convenient and reliable short cuts when possible.

The situation, of course, is different for some commercial operators, particularly those with specialist crops.

Quality of Water

Household water is usually quite suitable for hydroponics but, if there is any doubt, its mineral content should be checked by consulting the local Department of Agriculture. A salt level of greater than 250 parts per million will probably prevent the water being successfully used in hydroponics by the amateur. In such a situation one would have to use rainwater from a tank if it were available.

If your water has a high chlorine level, this may be reduced by exposing it to sunlight in an open tank. The result of this treatment may be assessed by using a standard swimming pool test kit.

Hydroponics can maximise the yield from rainwater in an arid region, especially if a recycling system is used.

Testing Nutrient Solutions

Electroconductivity

You can buy conductivity meters which will measure the total strength of a nutrient solution. They work on the principle that the higher the

HYDROHINT
An electroconductivity meter is a good investment and will improve your results. These little instruments also impress visitors and make everything more scientific.

mineral concentration, the lower the resistance to the passage of an electric current. Electroconductivity or E.C. is expressed as millisiemens/square centimetre and most nutrient solutions should be about 2. A nutrient level which has risen sufficiently to give an E.C. reading of 4 or more will cause deterioration of the plant.

Other units of electroconductivity may be used. A common one is conductivity factor units, or C.F. units and 10 C.F. units equal 1 millisiemen/square centimetre. Parts per million (p.p.m.) is another one: 700 P.P.M. = 10 C.F. units = 1 millisiemen/square centimetre. In this book I tend to use C.F. units since my meters are calibrated in these units.

Electroconductivity does not indicate the ratio of the various nutrients present but is merely a guide to their total concentration. Electroconductivity meters are vital pieces of equipment for commercial growers who must monitor their nutrient solution most closely, but in the first edition of this book I did not advise the amateur hydroponicer to purchase one. Now that efficient

and inexpensive meters are readily available their purchase should be considered, especially by those setting up a circulating hydroponic system. It only takes a jiffy to check the nutrient concentration and top it up if necessary. As well as instantly benefiting fast growing plants, it's interesting and fun to be better informed about the nutrient mix you are offering them.

Testing for pH

The pH of a solution signifies its degree of acidity or alkalinity. A neutral solution has a pH of 7, higher than 7 is alkaline and below 7 is acidic. Most plants are comfortable when fed a nutrient solution of pH 5.5 to 6.5 which is slightly acidic.

When a nutrient mixture is dissolved in water the pH usually settles around pH 6.3 which is ideal. If the pH becomes too high or too low, the

TESTING THE NUTRIENT MIX

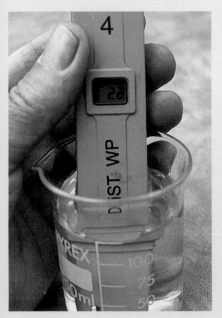

A A simple electroconductivity (E.C.) meter showing a conductivity factor (C.F.) reading of 22.

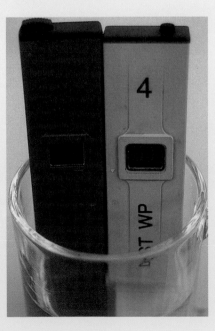

B Testing rainwater with a simple pH and E.C. meter: readings pH 6.8 and C.F. 00.

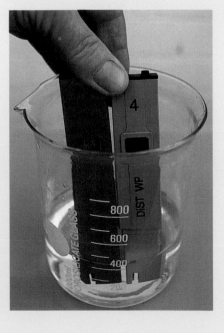

C Testing nutrient solution containing 2 grams of AquaGrow per litre (1/15 oz per 0.26 US gal): readings pH 6.3 and C.F. 29.

plants will take in less of various nutrients and deficiency states may develop. As seen in Table 4, there are optimum pH ranges for individual crops.

Accurate pH meters are an essential part of the monitoring equipment of the large-scale hydroponic establishments which keep the pH range to a very narrow limit to suit the particular crop being grown. Nearly always the pH gradually rises and monitoring allows the grower to control it by the careful addition of acid.

If you wish to lower the pH, then you can use domestic vinegar (acetic acid). On the rare occasions when the pH has got a little too high, I have just pumped it onto the garden and replaced it. This has only occurred when I have long delayed the scheduled replacement of nutrient solution.

An effective, but also a potentially hazardous, way to lower the pH is by using sulphuric acid (battery acid). Water should never be added to the acid as a violent reaction may occur. The acid must be added to water or the nutrient solution and rubber gloves, protective clothing and goggles should be worn to prevent injury. The use of this acid has a place in the strict maintenance of pH as required in large commercial hydroponic enterprises. It is not recommended for use by the domestic hydroponicer and I would never keep sulphuric acid in the home anyway.

Some commercial growers use phosphoric acid

THE DISCOVERY OF A GOOD MINERAL MIXTURE!

to control pH; this is a component in various preparations marketed as pH-lowering solutions.

Now that pH meters have also fallen in price and become simpler to use, their purchase can be considered but only after that of the E.C. meter. They are handy for checking the pH of soil in the garden in general, for example, checking that the soil around your azaleas is slightly acid. If it's not, say, between pH 5 and 6, give it some aluminium sulphate. To test the pH of soil, just put equal amounts of soil and water in a clean cup, stir well and lower in the probe or the detecting part of the pH meter. Use either distilled water or rainwater. After testing, make sure the meter probe is well washed with clean water. This is a good example of how the practice of hydroponics can indirectly benefit gardening in general.

In the practice of home hydroponics the pH range is usually between 6.0 and 6.5.

Preparation and Replacement of Nutrient Solutions

In non-recycling systems, the nutrient solution is made up as required, say enough to last a week according to the instructions on the packet. Most manufacturers include a plastic measure which, for example, might scoop up 2 gm (1/15 oz) of the preparation which is then added to 1 litre (0.26 US gal) of water.

Table 4 OPTIMUM pH RANGE FOR GROWTH OF SOME COMMON PLANTS			
pH 6.0–6.7	**pH 5.5–6.7**	**pH 5.2–6.7**	**pH 4.5–6.7**
Asparagus	Beans	Carrots	Potatoes
Beetroot	Broccoli	Radishes	
Cauliflower	Cabbage	Sweet corn	
Citrus	Celery	Tomatoes	
Parsnip	Cucumber	Turnip	
Rock melon	Lettuces		
Spinach	Onions		
Strawberries	Peas		

A A good commercial mixture (AquaGrow) which is highly soluble.

B The insoluble residue from a poor quality commercial hydroponic mixture.

HYDROHINTS

Nutrient solution is the perfect 'liquid fertiliser'. It can be used all around the garden from feeding young plants to encouraging a lemon tree. Don't make the solutions too strong; follow manufacturers' directions. If you have an electroconductivity meter, use it.

Usually the measures are of greater size and it may be advisable to use a large container and make up a week or so's supply of nutrient. This should be stored in an opaque bin to prevent algal growth. It's important to mark the precise water level required on the inside of the bin so that the correct concentration of nutrient can be made up easily.

Most good nutrient preparations dissolve up rapidly to completion or near completion. Hot water should never be added to the solids to help them dissolve as this will cause precipitation of calcium. Incidently, calcium may precipitate out of any nutrient solution if overheated when trapped in black plastic tubing. Apart from scorching the plants, this is another reason for keeping hydroponic solutions near room temperature.

It is important to check that an excessive amount of insoluble material is not present in the preparation. Occasionally, a product will be marketed which has been made of impure and low grade chemicals. Apart from blocking drippers and sprays, etc., such preparations may be roughly balanced and give poor results. I talk from bitter experience and now only use quality products.

Some manufacturers overcome the problem of minerals which don't dissolve easily, like calcium, as well as allowing for variation in composition, by producing two or even three pack mixes. These are generally only used in commercial and specialised hydroponics and care must be taken to follow precisely the manufacturer's instructions when using them.

An increasing variety of concentrated liquid nutrient solutions are being marketed. Many of these are in twin packs and, in some, the ratio of mixing one with another can be varied according to the stage of the crop being grown. Used properly these preparations can give excellent results. Whether one buys liquid nutrients or those in the dried form may be a personal choice or because a manufacturer of equipment provides or recommends a particular preparation. Some people find more satisfaction in scooping up a dried nutrient mixture than measuring out a concentrated liquid. This preference, which I tend towards, is a little hard to explain.

In a recycling system (see page 38) some people, myself included, use a half-strength solution. Until I used an E.C. meter, I would always add the same quantity of nutrient mixture two weeks later to bring it up to what I thought was near full strength. Two weeks further on, the whole lot would be pumped onto the garden and the cycle started again. After getting an E.C. meter, I found the nutrients were being quickly taken up and additions were required at least twice a week particularly in times of rapid growth, although early in the season once a fortnight was quite adequate. After six weeks, the system is still flushed onto the garden. Fresh water is then circulated to remove any mineral build up and also sprayed onto the garden.

> **HYDROHINT**
> To keep it in good condition open your main drum of hydroponic food only when necessary to fill a smaller container.

A two-pack liquid hydroponic preparation.

CHAPTER 3

Support Mediums for Hydroponic Plants

There are three main reasons why we replace soil with inert medium in hydroponics. First, although soil contains useful life such as certain bacteria and worms, it also harbours many enemies of plants. Apart from bacterial and fungal diseases the soil acts as a reservoir not only for insect pests at various stages of their life cycle, but also for the seeds of weeds or other unwanted plants. Second, since we are regularly supplying the required minerals via the nutrient solution those present in the earth are not needed. Third, the earth would be slowly washed away by the application of nutrient solution and a system which recycles the nutrient solution would end up with muddy water and blocked pipes and drippers.

A suitable medium to replace earth in hydroponics should have the following properties.

The medium should:
* have composition which gives adequate support for the root system and hence the plant;
* be stable and not break down;
* have the ability to absorb and hold moisture;
* be sufficiently porous to allow the circulation of air around the root system and have good drainage properties; and
* provide protection for the roots against extremes of temperature.

Let us consider some of the types of mediums that are in common use.

Bags of perlite and granulated growool with a growool slab in the foreground. The perlite bag weighs 8 kg (17 lb 10 oz) and the growool 12.5 kg (27 lb 8 oz).

Sand

This is one of the oldest materials used and it has the advantage of being inexpensive and usually in plentiful supply. It is long-lasting and is easy to keep clean. It should be coarse, as fine sand will drain poorly. Although wet sand is very heavy, little water penetrates into the grains so water retention is poor. The two disadvantages of sand are, therefore, its weight when wet and the speed with which it may dry out. Mr A. H. Sundstrom has had considerable success using this medium (see Bibliography).

Scoria

Scoria is used mainly in lightweight concrete construction, for example Nauru House in Melbourne. The hard red granules are of volcanic origin and absorb water by capillary action at a rate of 22 per

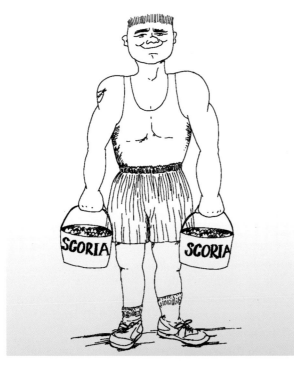

cent of their weight. Scoria is popular amongst many commercial growers because it is relatively inexpensive and has a long life. The usual size of the particles employed for hydroponics is from 5 to 10 mm (1/5 to 2/5 in) in diameter. Their porous nature allows adequate circulation of air. The main disadvantage of scoria is its heaviness.

Usually scoria comes complete with a fine red dust, which has to be washed away. This is best done on a lawn in the garden or in a gutter by pushing a garden hose to the bottom of the bucket and turning the water on at full pressure. Don't do it on a driveway as the fine red mud may later be walked into the house. You will find it will take at least ten minutes of washing to clear the red pigment. If you have a strong garden sieve with 4 mm (1/6 in) holes, this can be used instead of a bucket to hold the scoria while it is being washed.

Scoria has a part to play in home hydroponics provided one is muscular and there is a cheap source at hand.

Perlite

Perlite is a very useful medium, being extraordinarily light with high water-retention properties. It is manufactured when volcanic rock (aluminium silicate) is heated above 1000°C (1832°F) and it expands into sterile soft white inert particles. Those which are about 3 mm (1/8 in) in size are sold for hydroponic use as Perlite P500 in bags of 100 litres (26 US gal) which weigh only 8 kg (17 lb 10 oz). Smaller bags can be bought from nurseries, but this is less economic if you want to grow a lot of plants by hydroponics. Horticultural grade perlite is often unsuitable for hydroponics as it contains too much fine material.

Perlite is relatively stable, drains well and, although it has a high absorption rate of water (27 per cent), it is poorly permeated by minerals, which is an advantage. Because of its cost, it is rarely used in large commercial hydroponic units but finer grades of it are

Alyssum growing in sand.

Silverbeet growing in scoria.

employed extensively for raising seedlings and striking cuttings. The lightness and attractive appearance of perlite makes it popular for home hydroponics.

Care should be taken when handling fresh dry perlite as its fine dust has a high silica content which, if inhaled, is both irritating and potentially damaging to the lungs. To settle the dust, the required amount of dry perlite should be poured into a large plastic bag in the open air. Lightly spray inside the plastic bag with a garden hose while moving the contents about and it will become quite safe to handle. Don't add too much or the bag will become too heavy.

Some batches of perlite have an excess of fine material which may settle as sludge and block the drainage outlet of a container. The settling out effect can be reduced if you don't flood the container with too much liquid, as this encourages sedimentation. A good batch of perlite should produce very little sludge.

Although the problems perlite presents have been stressed, the reader should not be discouraged from using this versatile material. It is my second favourite after growool (see below).

A mixture of five parts of perlite to one of vermiculite is a wonderful combination and one I make great use of. If there are problems with the top layers drying out too much, a little extra vermiculite can be stirred into the mixture, thus increasing its water-holding capacity. This may increase the success rate, for example, when carrot seeds are planted.

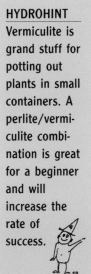

HYDROHINT
Vermiculite is grand stuff for potting out plants in small containers. A perlite/vermiculite combination is great for a beginner and will increase the rate of success.

Vermiculite

This medium has become much cheaper recently and is now about the same price as perlite. Like perlite, it is prepared by high temperature treatment of a mineral. Flakes of raw mica which contain silicates of aluminium and iron expand some twenty-fold and the very light soft glittering particles so formed

Below: Tomato and basil growing in perlite and Bottom: Tomato growing in vermiculite.

<u>A</u> Poinsettia and <u>B</u> chives and parsley in a vermiculite/perlite mixture — this little pig is ideal for the kitchen!

> **HYDROHINT**
> When dug into your garden, old vermiculite or perlite will improve soil quality.

can retain water some 50 per cent by volume. Most gardeners are familiar with the shiny golden brown appearance of vermiculite as it is often used in packaged seed-raising mixtures. The fine particles are ideal for keeping germinating seeds moist and protected.

For hydroponic use vermiculite is often mixed with scoria or perlite at a ratio of 1 to 5 or 1 to 10 to enhance the water-holding properties of the mixture. The disadvantage of vermiculite is that, unlike the other mediums described, it tends to break down over a year, which may lead to clogging of the tubing and the filters in a recycling system while, in simpler systems, drainage may be reduced leading to stagnation.

Growool (Horticultural Rock Wool)

The manufacture of this material in 1982 by CSR Bradford, Melbourne, was a significant event for the home hydroponic enthusiast. For some years we had read of a similar material gaining widespread support in Europe, especially in Holland and Demark. Commercial growers in those countries were using it for a variety of hydroponic cultures, including tomatoes, lettuce, cucumbers, cut flowers and plant propagation.

Growool is manufactured by heating a mixture of basalt rock, limestone and silica to 1600°C (2912°F). The molten slag is poured onto fast-spinning wheels which throw the material out as fibres. As the fibres are formed they are sprayed with binders and wetting agents and then cured in an oven. The yellow growool emerges from the oven compressed into rigid slabs.

Growool is extremely light, 1 cubic metre (0.76 cu yd) weighing only 80 kg (176 lb), and it can be cut into any shape with a sharp knife. It is inorganic, sterile, inert and won't bind any chemicals to its structure. Growool has an extraordinarily high water- and air-holding capacity as it takes up some 80 per cent of water and 17 per cent of air.

This relatively cheap material is marketed as propagating blocks, wrapped cubes or large growing slabs (see photographs). Seeds or seedlings

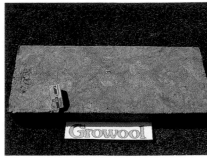

A dry growool slab.

Commercial production of tomatoes using growool slabs. The roots will extend into the slab from the wrapped cube. (*Courtesy Ric Donnan*)

Chives growing on growool slabs.

HYDROHINT
Make sure the container is strong enough to hold the medium, particularly when it is wet.

can be introduced into the top one-quarter of a propagation block and later, when the plants are big enough, the block can be lowered into a larger wrapped cube. The wrapped cube can subsequently be placed on a growing slab and the root system will extend into the slab.

A special advantage of growool is that plants can easily be shuffled around from one place to another. For example, herbs growing in a block can be brought into the kitchen for usage over a few days and then replaced in the hydroponic system. The same can be done with lettuces.

Blocks of flowers can be brought inside for temporary display before returning them to the system.

Growool is non-toxic and safe for immediate use, which is an obvious advantage for a busy person. Initially, when growool is washed, a yellow frothy solution appears which is neutral and quite harmless. Some people, however, have been alarmed at the sudden but temporary frothing which occurs when new slabs are introduced into a recycling hydroponic system.

When growool has been soaked with water its pH (see page 13) will be about 7. Prior to planting seedlings it is best to saturate the growool with half-strength nutrient solution as this will bring the pH down to about 6.3, which is the preferred level for most plants.

Two problems are common when growool slabs are used. Because of the high water-retention rate, it is essential either to have very good drainage or to avoid using too much nutrient solution. If the roots of a plant are kept waterlogged, the plant will slowly drown.

Good drainage of a growool slab can be obtained by placing the supporting tray at an angle of some 15 degrees. The alternative is to have a series of drainage holes immediately under a horizontal slab so the nutrient solution can drain thoroughly prior to recycling. Some commercial growers who do not recycle their nutrients merely apply the nutrient solution to the growool slab and allow the excess to drain away. Unless the quantities of nutrient solution are accurately dispensed this practice may be uneconomic and environmentally unsound.

The other problem is more one of aesthetics than inferior plant growth. The upper surface of growool slabs often becomes covered with ugly dark algae or even moss. This can be avoided by a cover of opaque plastic sheeting or by placing slabs of plastic foam around the plants. The manufacturers now have available, as an option, slabs prewrapped in opaque plastic.

Skin Irritation by Growool

Although this material is non-toxic, some irritation of the skin may occur when handling the dry material. Immediate relief is obtained by washing the area with running water. Growool contains little spikes which can sometimes penetrate the skin and these instantly soften when the material is wetted.

Granulated Growool

This material, which is a by-product of growool manufacture, came on sale in 1984. Previously it was either recycled in the growool factory or discarded. To my mind it is an extremely promising

Garden pot filled with granulated growool.

Conifer in container filled with expanded clay balls. This has been the family Christmas tree for a number of years and it seems to have 'bonsaied' itself.

and versatile medium. Granulated growool is of identical composition to growool and comes in packs weighing 12.5 kg (27 lb 8 oz). A fluffy material, it is easily handled and currently is used mainly commercially for propagation. I have found it ideal for use in deeper containers such as plastic buckets and it has proven the best medium for tomatoes.

Expanded Clay Balls

Special materials such as expanded clay balls, as used in the Luwasa plant system, are very popular in Europe and are now available in Australia. These balls are made by baking specially prepared clay in ovens at 1200°C (2192°F). The clay expands and the final product is hard but porous and allows good entry of both water and air. Incidentally, 'sharp granules' of expanded clay are manufactured in Australia but these are not suitable for hydroponics. They are used for absorbing industrial wastes like motor oil in garages.

Expanded clay is successfully used in many simple hydroponic systems. The overseas manufacturers of expanded clay balls have a number of agents in Australia which market a variety of small but complete kits (see expanded clay under hydroponic suppliers in the Appendix). Some of these kits are most ingenious in their design and operation. Expanded clay balls complement these small hydroponic systems but until recently were too expensive in Australia for use in the larger containers required for most home hydroponics.

Other Mediums

A variety of other mediums has been described elsewhere, but often they are difficult to use. In some places, sawdust has been a success; however, it is not recommended for the amateur because of drainage, uptake of nutrients and disease problems. It is not inert and breakdown commences quickly.

Some plastics have been used as mediums and the writer used polystyrene pellets in a vertical strawberry tube during one season. The water-holding capacity of such plastic is very low and the experts recommend that a very weak soapy solution should be flushed through the system at the beginning to increase water absorption. They also suggest that 30 per cent perlite and 20 per cent vermiculite should be added to the polystyrene pellets. For efficiency and lightness, nothing to date has approached a perlite (70 per cent)/vermiculite (30 per cent) mix or granulated growool for performance.

Foam substrates made from polyurethane particles of different densities and sizes which are compressed into blocks are gaining popularity in Europe. This medium, which is also known as bonded foam, is marketed by the manufacturers under the name of Aggrofoam. It is proving increasingly popular, particularly in Holland and in England where it is known as Richgrow. It

> **HYDROHINT**
> Avoid spilling expanded clay balls on your back lawn. They take a lot of picking up!

Table 5 SOME ADVANTAGES AND DISADVANTAGES OF MEDIUMS

	COST	WEIGHT	LIFE	WATER	VERSATILITY
Sand	low	very high	years	very poor	moderate
Scoria	low	very high	years	moderate	moderate
Perlite	high	moderate*	1–3 years	high	high
Vermiculite	high	moderate*	1–2 years	high	high
Growool slabs	high	high*	years	very high	very high
Growool, granulated	moderate	moderate*	years	very high	very high

* wet weight

seems a promising medium as its life may be up to fifteen years, after which it can be recycled. Care must be taken in establishing plants in Aggrofoam because it tends to dry out faster than, say, growool. Once the plants are under way, they apparently do very well providing feeding is regular. I have no experience as yet with this product.

What Medium Should One Use?

At hydroponic meetings sometimes very dogmatic or even heated opinions are aired by proponents of a particular medium. The joy of hydroponics is the degree of individual experimentation that can be conducted in the privacy of your back garden. Keep an open mind and determine what medium or medium combination is most suitable for your own needs. Visit as many hydroponic units as possible and always be prepared to try something new.

Currently I am using well-drained growool either as slabs or in granulated form for most crops and perlite for root crops like carrots or parsnips (see Epilogue).

CHAPTER 4

Types of Hydroponic Systems

Containers and Fittings for Hydroponic Systems

The keen hydroponicer keeps an eagle eye open for any container which might be used effectively to hold medium and nutrient solution, or for water-filled heat banks (see Chapter 7). There has been no better time to take up hydroponics because of today's abundance of plastic products, many of which are destined to end up as rubbish. Metal containers are generally useless because they require protection from contact with nutrient solution. Likewise, metal fittings should be avoided although the odd brass fitting is sometimes unavoidable and seems fairly stable.

The introduction of many plastic plumbing fittings has been a great help, as they are stable, easy to use and relatively inexpensive. *Plastic guttering* makes containers of any length. The guttering together with the 'U'-shaped end bits can be bought from plumbers suppliers.

Cheap *plastic laundry buckets* make ideal

> **HYDROHINT**
> In hot weather and/or when extensive foliage is dependent on feeding, additional recycling of nutrient may be necessary.

KEEP IT SIMPLE!

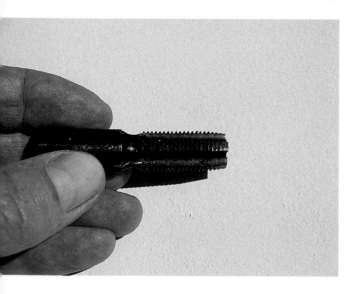

Left: Plastic bucket with young beetroot in perlite.

Middle left: Fitting outlets to plastic containers—for A$10 the lot, these 25 litre (1.7 US gal) used containers were a good buy from a local cake shop.

Below: Plastic pipe used as a container for leeks and strawberries.

Left:
CONNECTING OUTLETS TO PLASTIC CONTAINERS:
Method 1
The thread-making tool described in the text.

CONNECTING OUTLETS TO PLASTIC CONTAINERS: Method 2

A̲ A hole is made with a hot soldering iron.

B̲ Silicone is applied liberally.

C̲ The fitting is pushed home firmly. In this case there is a plastic nut which is then screwed on from the inside.

containers for all but the smallest of plants. Their handles allow them to be suspended and they can be arranged in tiers with each one draining into the one below. Holes can easily be drilled in them and, if you use a suitable thread-making tool, plastic outlets can be screwed in tightly.

Some plastic containers shatter when drilled or are too thin to take a thread. Such problems can generally be solved by making holes with a hot soldering iron. When cool, usually the waste plastic can easily be scraped away and the fitting made watertight by the use of copious quantities of a silicone sealant instead of screwing in the connection. Allow a full day for the sealant to harden and become waterproof (see the photographs).

An alternative is to use double-flanged grommets to make a leak-proof connection. This sounds very technical but it is not. The grommet is a little rubber gadget which, when squeezed into a hole in the plastic container, allows the rigid outlet to be tightly fitted. To be successful the hole must be precisely the recommended size and the grommet and outlet pipe must be, as it were, made for each other (see the photographs on page 28).

An important advantage of buckets over larger containers is that they are easily moved about, for example, from a shady area when the plant is first established to a region of full light when rapid growth is required.

A simple non-recycling system can be made using a bottle and a *plastic box* (see the photographs

CONNECTING OUTLETS TO PLASTIC CONTAINERS: <u>Method 3</u>
Use of double-flanged grommets (if you can obtain these and the plastic containers are of good quality this method is the quickest and most reliable).

<u>A</u> Double-flanged rubber grommet with connecting piece (purchased from Plastic Plumbing and Irrigation Supplies).

<u>B</u> Make an appropriately, sized hole for the grommet as recommended by the manufacturer (in this case a 16 mm (5/8 in) drill worked perfectly).

<u>C</u> Push the grommet fully into the hole.

<u>D</u> Rigid tubing is then inserted to give a leak-proof fitting.

on page 29). A washed orange juice container had a 3 mm (1/8 in) hole punched in its lid, and was then filled with nutrient solution, inverted and put in the plastic box. The nutrient solution seeped out of the container keeping the bottom of the plastic box flooded with nutrient. The plastic box was then filled with a 1/5 mixture of perlite and vermiculite and, in this case, radish seeds were introduced into the system. The orange juice container was refilled with nutrient solution once a fortnight.

Foam plastic window boxes are ideal for the hydroponic growing of lettuces, herbs and, of course, flowers. Establishing a hydroponic garden in these containers is exactly the same as with the bucket system (pages 25–7). They are equally suited to non-recycling and recycling systems. They provide excellent insulation from excessive heat and are strong enough to support any saturated medium. However,

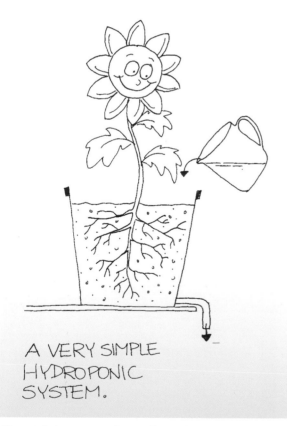

A VERY SIMPLE
HYDROPONIC
SYSTEM.

The nutrient saturates the medium and the excess drains away and is lost. If you make the drainage hole several centimetres from the bottom, a small reservoir of nutrient solution will remain at the bottom of the container.

A SIMPLE NON-RECYCLING SYSTEM

<u>A</u> A washed orange juice container and plastic box.

<u>B</u> Container filled with perlite/vermiculite mixture.

<u>C</u> Six weeks after radish seeds were sprinkled on the surface harvesting commenced.

A FOAM PLASTIC WINDOW BOX

<u>A</u> Basic requirements.

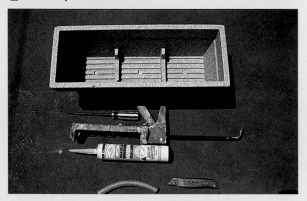

<u>B</u> Make a hole for the outlet tubing with a screwdriver or knife and cut down the transverse ribs to allow drainage. Use silicone to anchor the drainage tube and seal exit area.

<u>C</u> External part of drainage tube showing silicone seal.

<u>D</u> Cover the tube with a thin layer of growool to allow good drainage (other materials can be used such as gauze, shadecloth or panty hose).

<u>E</u> A 5 to 1 mixture of perlite and vermiculite is made using a large plastic bag.

<u>F</u> The window box filled with media is now ready to receive plants or seeds.

G This box was used for growing salad vegetables.

H A second box was used for flowers.

I This photograph of more advanced flowers shows the drainage system.

great care is required if you want to move them when they are filled with the heavier mediums. Before you do any modifications to one, half fill it with water, because some of them have cracks which can be annoying. If a window box leaks, return it to the store unless you can seal the leak yourself.

It's very easy to use a small knife to make a drainage hole in one of these boxes but very difficult to cut the hole neatly, and usually a silicone sealant must be used if you want to make a waterproof join to a hose. Some of the boxes have several transverse lower ribs which have to be planed down with a sharp knife, otherwise they may retard drainage. The volume of a box which measures 1 metre by 14 cm by 12 cm (39 1/3 in by 5 1/2 in by 4 1/2 in) is about twice that of a 9 litre (2.3 US gal) laundry bucket (pages 25–7) and so double the quantities of medium and nutrient solution will be required.

Some examples of the use of these containers are seen in the photographs.

Black polythene sausages hung vertically and filled with a lightweight medium are superb containers for growing strawberries. Details of their construction and use are described in the section on strawberries in Chapter 6.

One can make use of any bits and pieces and improvise as they come to hand or sail ahead and purchase the exact containers and fittings to construct a carefully planned unit.

Non-recycling Systems

A very simple system is best for beginners and allows them to get the feel of hydroponics. All one needs is a few well-drained containers, be they clean plant pots or buckets, filled with medium. The roots of the plant should be carefully washed with fresh water before it is gently planted (Chapter 5). Nutrient solution can be prepared in a watering can and the plant fed at regular intervals depending upon the retentive properties of the medium (Chapter 7). Excess solution drains away from the container and is lost (see the picture on page 29).

A WICK SYSTEM

This is excellent for a patio as many plants can be grown in this way.

A Basic requirements are an inner and outer vessel and a wick (in this case a plastic pot was made to fit snugly into a white plastic container by removing all but the rim of the container's lid and the wick was a length of cord purchased from a fabric shop).

B The interior wall of the container was painted with black plastic paint to keep light out and prevent the growth of algae which, apart from being unsightly, will use up nutrients.

C A knot was tied so the wick wouldn't slip through the hole in the plant pot and the wick fitted to the inner chamber.

D Some granulated growool was placed at the bottom of the pot to help retain media and it was filled with a perlite/vermiculite mixture.

This principle is used in many of the successful commercial hydroponic concerns. They have accurately determined the exact amount of solution required and at what intervals it should be released into the containers. By providing only freshly constituted nutrient solution they avoid the problems of recycling, but very accurate calculations are required to avoid wastage of minerals and overwatering.

There are many variations of non-recycling systems, which the beginner can try (see Chapter 9). One that is becoming popular is using a growool slab simply encased in plastic or in a box.

If it is not overwatered and/or is sloped to allow good drainage, plant growth should be excellent.

Some of the hydroponic equipment outlets are now selling a range of simple kits which serve as useful introductions to hydroponics. In addition, some plant pots are marketed which are fitted with a wick and reservoir for watering (see the picture). Although they are primarily used for plants growing normally in soil, they can give good results using medium and nutrient solution. The nutrient solution is drawn up by the wick into the medium, thus keeping it moist.

E The tomato plant's roots were washed carefully prior to planting.

F This is the established plant two months later.

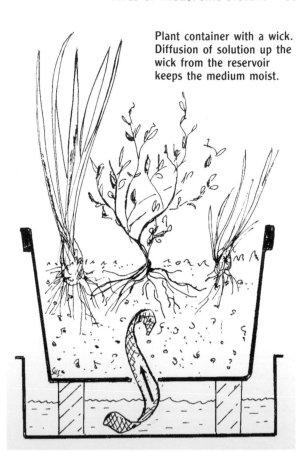

Plant container with a wick. Diffusion of solution up the wick from the reservoir keeps the medium moist.

Setting up a Wick System

The photographs show how a wick system can be used to grow cherry tomatoes successfully. It was too late in the season to obtain young plants, so it proved a good example of how an advanced plant can be successfully transferred from its normal earth medium to a hydroponic system.

The Auto-pot

Jim Fah's 'Smart-valve' — automation without electricity

The development of the Smart-valve looks set to give home hydroponics a great boost. This ingenious device releases nutrient fluid until it reaches a depth of some 30 mm (1 1/6 in) but does not allow the escape of further nutrient fluid until the plants have taken up nearly all the liquid. Because it does not maintain a stagnant pool of nutrient fluid at a constant level it mimics to some extent the flood and drain system.

The story of the Auto-pot's development and application is one of both inspiration and tenacity. In 1981 its inventor, an agricultural scientist called Jim Fah, was working in Malaysia raising gloxinia, beautiful flowering plants from Brazil, which need constant attention. Since he had to be away sometimes for several weeks, a method of regular feeding had to be devised.

The idea of a device which would automatically release water or nutrient solution to a predetermined level was born. It was only to release the fluid when the plant had nearly used up the volume which had previously flowed through the valve. It was to be fed by gravity or pressure from a water tap using a reducing valve. The first Smart-valve was granted a USA patent in 1985 and, after a great deal of further developmental work, the current Smart-valve received a USA patent in 1989. It now has patents pending in many other countries. It's a great success story — Jim has now sold more than 20 000 Smart-valves and their sales are rising dramatically as many more uses for this device are found.

> **HYDROHINT**
> The purchase of a good kit using the nutrient film technique is worth serious consideration.

> **HYDROHINT**
> Protect nutrient solutions from sunlight otherwise algal growth will occur.

The Smart-valve and Auto-pot system have won a number of awards including the Inventors Association of Victoria, Australia, first prize 1992 and the best Victorian invention at the Royal Melbourne Show of that same year.

How does the Smart-valve work? It consists of two chambers which interact as if you were lowering a drinking glass into a bucket of water. When you invert the glass and raise it to near the surface, it will remain filled with water. However, lift it a fraction higher so air can enter and the contents of the glass flows out.

The current Smart-valves only open when the nutrient level surrounding them has dropped to zero. This prevents stagnation and allows aeration of the plant roots prior to the arrival of fresh nutrient solution to the pre-set level. The rise and fall of nutrient solution offers enormous advantages to hydroponic plants.

As long as there is nutrient being fed by gravity from a tank, the cycle can be repeated indefinitely. If the plants are growing faster in warm weather and their demands are greater, these will be supplied automatically. There are obviously many other uses for this valve in the controlling of the flow of various liquids, not only in horticulture but in industry in general.

The Smart-valve is virtually maintenance free. It is probably one of the most environmentally friendly inventions in many years as its energy requirements are near zero, being fed by gravity alone and needing no timing system and no electric power. Best of all, no nutrient or water runs away to waste.

Uses of the Smart-valve

Initially Jim Fah started to develop suitable systems to incorporate the Smart-valve. There were some hiccups in design and function early on but generally these various kits are well worth considering (see purchasing a hydroponic kit, page 49). Although the quality control is very good, as with any purchase it is wise to set up the kit and test the Smart-valve as soon as possible. Plain water can be used for the test. Speaking of plain water, it is only fair to mention that some of the earlier Smart-valves played up because their innards became gummed up with material that had precipitated out of the nutrient solution. It is important to use only best quality nutrients and to maintain effective filtration (see Care of Auto-pot systems, below).

Also the Smart-valves may occasionally stick in the open position and cause flooding, but this is rare and further improvements made in 1995 should considerably reduce the risk. The latest containers have an overflow outlet and a bucket placed under the outlet should prevent accidents.

Auto-pot systems are suitable both for beginners and for those who require larger and more ambitious set-ups. They are particularly valuable for use in areas where electricity is not available or would be too expensive to install.

They are especially attractive for primary and secondary schools, as they will look after themselves during the school holidays and the students may learn some elementary science from the story of the Smart-valve.

<u>Above:</u> Smart-valve and (<u>inset</u>) its inventor Jim Fah. (*Courtesy Jim Fah*)

<u>Above right:</u> The giant twin-walled Auto-pot unit is ideal for patios. (The container holds 50 litres (13.2 US gal) of nutrient solution, which will keep most plants going for many months.) After three months these petunias had only used two-thirds of the nutrient solution provided. Seeing Kelly and Jane beside the pot gives an idea of its large capacity.

<u>Right:</u> A fine display of miniature petunias growing in an Auto-pot.

SUCCESS WITH SMART-VALVES

<u>A</u> A hanging basket viewed from above; the Smart-valve is fitted in the lower section.

<u>B</u> A vermiculite/perlite mixture is layered over a bottom layer of vermiculite.

<u>C</u> Here Jenny is admiring a fern and petunia combination. Miniature carnations are growing in the basket attached to the wall.

<u>D</u> Chillies fed with Smart-valve.

<u>E</u> Vegetable display at Jim Fah's headquarters.

<u>F</u> These beautiful orchids (cymbidiums) fed with the Smart-valve won first prize at an orchid show in Florida, USA.

(*Photos D, E and F courtesy Jim Fah*)

Systems available from Auto-pot

The Smart-valve is the heart of all the Auto-pot systems. The nutrient is fed to the Smart-valve either by gravity from various sized tanks or directly from a water tap. In the latter instance, a pressure regulator must be provided and the tap water injected with the appropriate amount of concentrated nutrient through a special device.

1 The Auto-pot starter kit

This kit consists of a grow box of polystyrene which may be deep or shallow. The kit includes liquid nutrient, a Smart-valve, a 10 litre (2.6 US gal) tank, filter and connecting tubing, etc. The polystyrene becomes porous so this kit is unsuitable for use in the house. Examples of the use of this kit are seen in the photographs.

Note: Unlike the tanks provided with the larger kits, this tank is translucent and algae may grow in the nutrient solution and cause blockages. The tank should be protected from sunlight either by a cardboard box or black plastic film.

2 Automatic hydropak

This is a more solid construction of greater capacity. It has a heavy plastic growing tray and the inserts provided are for either four 25 cm (10 in) pots or six 15 cm (6 in) pots. The pots are supplied, as is everything else required other than seedlings or seeds. This is an ideal unit for balconies or flats, etc. where space is at a premium, and can be used indoors provided a tray is placed under it in case of accidents. It is hard not to get good results with this unit.

Jim continues to invent more devices to improve his systems. For example, the grow tray in garden systems can be fitted with what is called an automatic Smart-siphon. This cuts in when there has been a lot of rain which could waterlog the plants. It is activated by excess water and reduces the water level in the unit to 10 per cent of the normal maximum. Thus, when the weather is wet and the plants need less moisture, the adjustment is made automatically.

3 The carefree hanging garden kit

This system will appeal to many gardeners. The kit provides six hanging pots, all with built in Smart-valves, and the system connects directly to a garden tap and includes a device for the automatic injection of fertiliser. When installed and running properly, not only should the plants thrive spectacularly, but one does not have the problem of water dripping and staining the surfaces of balconies and patios. Moreover, the baskets can be higher than usual since gardeners do not have to struggle to raise watering cans high above their heads. For those who find gardening physically difficult or whose time for gardening is very limited, this hanging hydroponic garden can be bliss.

Other products from Auto-pot range from window box and wall sets to equipment designed for quite extensive Auto-pot systems, including commercial production. Auto-pot (see Appendix) should be contacted for further details.

Care of Auto-pot systems

Filters should be checked regularly. The more foreign material in the water, the more often will it be necessary for them to be cleaned. Usually once a month is adequate. To check, disconnect the filter from the line and note the amount of water coming out from the tube which would normally go into the filter. If this is much more than the flow that has been coming through the filter, then backwashing is obviously necessary. Clean the filter by connecting it back to front (not to the system!) and allowing water to run through it for five minutes. Then replace it as it was originally after checking the flow rate through it has improved.

Accessible Smart-valves should be thoroughly washed every eight weeks or so to keep them free of sediment and other foreign matter. However, they need careful handling as it is very easy to upset the function of the valve. It is especially important not to flood them when setting up the system, as this seems to stop them opening to let in more nutrient.

> **HYDROHINT**
> When starting hydroponics, begin on a small scale and don't overcrowd your plants.

FLOOD AND DRAIN SYSTEMS

<u>A</u> Flood and drain system available from One Stop Sprinklers.

<u>B</u> Flood and drain system with eggplant growing in clay balls.

<u>C</u> Bob Campbell's flood and drain system growing vegetables.

Recycling Systems

The reasons why most home hydroponic systems recycle nutrient solution are to conserve the nutrient, to keep the area reasonably dry and, in more expensive systems, to escape some of the sheer hard work and monotony of regular feeding by using an electric pump. **Last, but not least, water is not wasted.**

Manual Methods

To recycle nutrient one obviously has to collect it first from the plant container. The simplest method is to place a large dish under the container and pour the contents back over the plant from time to time (see Chapter 7).

A little less simple to set up is a container with an outlet and hose fitted a little way from its base (see the picture). Nutrient mixed, say, in a watering can is poured into the container and the liquid in the can is drained into the receptacle by gravity. This simple system, or variations on it, is ideal for beginners who want to get the feel of nutrient recycling.

It is good fun if only a few containers are in use and they are not large, but can be not only a watery experience but quite hard labour when conducted on a large scale. Nevertheless, provided the quantity of solution that has to be lifted is kept as small as possible and you have time to repeat the operation, sometimes twice daily in hot weather, then this technique is an inexpensive and rewarding way to enjoy hydroponics. Over the years, various systems have been developed, using pulleys and winches, to lift the drained nutrient solution to the required level. However, with the availability of electric pumps which are inexpensive to run, such techniques have gone out of fashion, except in areas of some developing countries where there is no electric power.

A simple flood and drain system is also popular and easily managed on a small scale (see the photographs). Some excellent commercial kits are available which use a submersible electric pump. A timer switch activates the pump at regular intervals, and the container, usually in the form of a large flat tray, is flooded to a depth of several centimetres (say an inch) before the pump cuts out. The nutrient solution then drains back to the nutrient reservoir, the whole process being repeated in an hour or so.

In 1983 I developed a device called a *hydrotube* (see the pictures on pages 40–1) which allows a very simple recycling of nutrients and has proved popular for growing herbs and flowers. Since that time, I've come across lots of variations of this 'invention', many of which pre-dated it. The reader may have some fun making something along the lines described.

The system consists of a vertical plastic cylinder containing granulated growool or a perlite/vermiculite mixture. Other media can be used but these

Container with an outlet and hose.

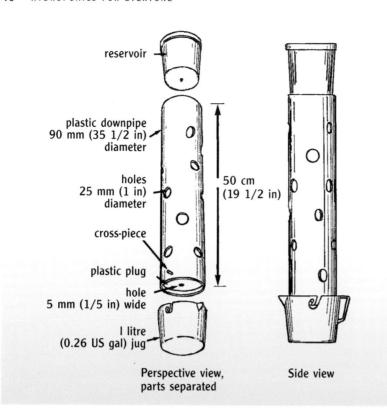

reservoir

plastic downpipe
90 mm (35 1/2 in)
diameter

holes
25 mm (1 in)
diameter

50 cm
(19 1/2 in)

cross-piece

plastic plug

hole
5 mm (1/5 in) wide

I litre
(0.26 US gal) jug

**Perspective view,
parts separated**

Side view

The hydrotube

work best. Holes are cut at intervals around the cylinder and seeds, bulbs or seedlings carefully planted next to the holes inside it. A reservoir inside the device permits the slow release of the solution, which runs down the tube to a small jug at the lower end. When the jug is full simply detach it from the lower end and pour the mixture into the reservoir at the top, thus starting the system all over again (see Chapter 7). The hydrotube has the advantage of good drainage, simplicity and a large surface area for the growing of plants.

To make my hydrotube you will need a length of plastic downpiping some 50 cm (19 1/2 in) in length and 90 mm (35 1/2 in) in diameter. The lower end should be sealed with a plastic plug, available from most plumbers' suppliers. A hole 5 mm (1/5 in) wide should be drilled in the centre of the plug for drainage and a number of holes about 25 mm (1 in) wide should be made in the cylinder for the insertion of plants, seeds or bulbs (see the picture). A 1 litre (0.26 US gal) jug must be attached underneath to collect the nutrient. A simple way to do this is to insert a thin crosspiece

through close fitting holes in the pipe. Then use nail scissors to cut 'J'-shaped holes on both sides of the jug to fit the crosspiece (see the pictures).

Lastly, wedge another container onto the top of the tube to act as a reservoir. Any suitably shaped plastic container can be used. Make a small hole in the centre of its base to release the nutrient solution slowly into the tube.

Alternatively, you can make a polythene tube which fits inside the cylinder. Pack the bottom three-quarters of the tube with growool and leave the top one-quarter empty to act as a reservoir for the nutrient solution. Use a sharp knife or scissors to cut round holes in the polythene where there are holes in the plastic cylinder so that the medium is exposed and you can plant the seeds or plants. I find that this method, using a polythene tube, is easier and works just as well.

Before planting the hydrotube, a few litres of water should be run through it and discarded. The roots of the plants should then be washed carefully and very gently inserted into the medium. A pencil can be used for opening up the medium and firming it around the plants. The hydrotube should be kept in a cool place out of direct sunlight for several days while the plants become established.

The jug is filled with half-strength nutrient solution which is poured into the hydrotube. Refix the jug immediately to the bottom of the hydrotube to collect the solution as it runs through. In mild weather the nutrient solution should be recycled every third or fourth day. When the plants are larger and/or the weather is hot this should be done daily. Plants will take up a lot of water at this stage and, as water is evaporated from the nutrient mixture, fresh water must be added to top up the jug before recycling. This keeps the mixture at relatively the same strength.

Once a fortnight the nutrient solution should be replaced. Every two months several litres (or gallons) of fresh water should be run through the hydrotube to remove any build-up of minerals. Most plants should be cut back regularly to ensure continued growth of fresh foliage.

Delightful floral displays or copious herb productions are easily achieved with these tubes.

If you don't want to go to the bother of making a hydrotube a beautiful device called the *Green Genii* is now available. Reasonably priced, these units work well and are a good hydroponic starting point (see the photographs on page 42).

Recycling Systems Using Electric Pumps

Corrosion-resistant submersible electric pumps act as the heart of many amateur hydroponic gardens. The pump sits at the bottom of the drainage tank and circulates the nutrient solution through the hydroponic system, either continuously or at predetermined intervals. Such pumps allow the nutrient solution to be raised several metres (or feet) to flow through the plant containers and back to the holding tank or reservoir. A basic recycling system is shown in the picture. There are infinite varieties of arrangements which can be devised by the amateur and many show great ingenuity in the use of materials available.

It is possible to use aquarium pumps designed to move air to raise the nutrient solution up to the hydroponic plants. In some the air pressure produced by the pump forces the nutrient solution

THE HYDROTUBE

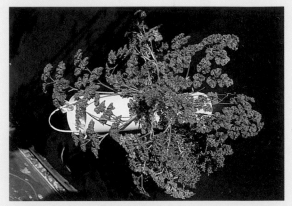

A Hydrotube growing parsley.

B The same hydrotube from above.

C Chives emerging from the side of a hydrotube.

GREEN GENII

<u>A</u> Green Genii kit.

<u>B</u> Just planted with sweet William, lobelia and alyssum.

<u>C</u> Green Genii floral display four weeks later.

upwards and out of a sealed container, while others rely on rising bubbles of air to elevate the nutrient solution through vertical tubing. Quite ingenious use is made of this type of aquarium pump in some hydroponic devices but generally they are small scale systems of moderate productivity. No doubt there will be further developments using these little air pumps, particularly since they aerate the nutrient solution as part of the recycling process.

However, it is the improvement in liquid pumping electric pumps which have given hydroponics a boost. These range from tiny (and cheap) water-moving aquarium pumps to swimming pool pumps. There are a number of home hydroponic kits available which include electric pumps. It is important to compare what is available before purchasing one and advice from a hydroponic society should be sought if in doubt

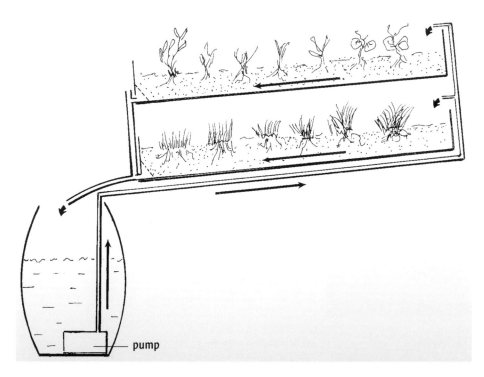

A basic recycling system using a submersible electric pump.

or if there is no opportunity to examine the kit before purchase by mail order.

Electric pumps

When describing these, I deliberately called them 'the heart of the system'. If they fail then the whole hydroponic garden can be in jeopardy. Unfortunately, some prove not to be corrosion-resistant, although sold as such. Many have been designed as garden fountain pumps and not manufactured to withstand contact with nutrient minerals. They must be checked to ensure that only plastic and no metal other than stainless steel will be in contact with the nutrient solution. It's a good idea to ask to inspect the impeller (driving spindle) and its chamber before purchase. It is also very important to discover the height to which the pump can raise water. Some barely reach 1 metre (3 ft 3 in) whereas for most hydroponic systems at least 1.5 metres (4 ft 11 in) is required.

Electric pumps are liable to burn out or wear out. They should never be allowed to run when they are not pumping nutrient solution and filters should be installed to ensure that medium particles do not enter them. Vermiculite, for example, can

be very abrasive to a pump's moving parts. Some people install two pumps (one spare) because the whole hydroponic system is so dependent on the pump for regular nutrient. It is cheaper to service the pump frequently at times when plant growth is at its slowest.

I have had trouble with a number of pumps over the years. In a small unit the little submersible fountain pumps have performed well provided they are serviced annually. Other good and often cheaper little pumps are now available. For my big hydroponics unit I have a non-submersible swimming pool pump which gives a performance that brings joy to my heart. The excess nutrient solution is returned directly to the reservoir and so is not a problem and, in fact, assists in the aeration (see Epilogue). Commercial hydroponic systems generally use large pumps placed outside the drainage tanks, but such pumps are usually of greater capacity than required by the amateur. Whatever the make and type of pump, a plan of routine maintenance should be in place to reduce the chances of a hydroponic disaster.

The pump must be installed safely and the use of extension cords should be avoided if possible by

A simple installation showing the position of a submersible electric pump and a ball valve. In this case the ball valve was connected to an overhead water tank. If it were connected directly to a water main, either a pressure reducing valve or high pressure hosing would be necessary. Both are available from normal plumbing suppliers. All-plastic ball valves are now available which are preferable to using ones like this which has brass fittings.

having an electrician provide a power point. When the motors are controlled by a time clock, this should be waterproofed. Even in the best hydroponic system, sudden water spills can occur; hence the need to protect electric cables and connections from the risk of wetting which may lead to electrocution. The safety aspects of an electricity supply cannot be overstressed and bad planning or just carelessness can prove fatal, not only to hydroponic enthusiasts but to innocent bystanders. If you have any doubt about safety, do consult an electrician or your local electricity supply authority. Most of the larger commercial growers use only a 25 volt supply inside their greenhouses, which almost eliminates any risk.

At times I have been quite horrified to see amateur hydroponic enthusiasts using double adaptors to connect live cables which are actually lying on a very wet floor. All connections must be watertight and kept away from moisture as much as possible. Since the combination of water and electricity is so dangerous, it is strongly recommended that you have an electrician to install a safety cut out switch in the power supply to your hydroponic unit.

Having said all the above about the problems of submersible electric pumps I should stress that a good pump, safely installed and run by a time clock, allows automation of the hydroponic garden

so that you can relax at work knowing that your plants are all being well fed and growing like mad.

Setting up the system

Most gardening and hardware shops sell 10 metre (33 ft) coils of 13 mm (1/2 in) diameter black tubing and drippers for use in conventional irrigation systems. They also stock simple plastic filters which can be fitted into the tubing as well as elbow joints and connecting pieces.

It is very easy to connect up a basic recycling system. The plastic piping can be cut with scissors to the desired lengths and elbows only have to be used when sharp bends are required. Tighter fittings are achieved by briefly immersing the ends you want to join in hot water. When you have laid out the system the pump should be activated to make sure that the height the tubing reaches is not too high for the ability of the pump, i.e. liquid should be able to squirt out of the upper open end. The pump can then be turned off, the end sealed

HYDROHINT
Service your hydroponic pump regularly and never let it run dry.

with a plastic bung or folded over and taped down, and drippers inserted into the tubing wherever you want them.

There are many ways of inserting the drippers into the tubing as it crosses over the plant containers. The simplest and cheapest is to use the little plastic spikes which are sold by the dripper manufacturers. The spike makes a hole in the required spot in the tubing and the base of the dripper is pushed in fully and then pulled out a fraction so that it fits tightly against the inner wall of the tube. If the hole has been badly made and leaks, little repair plugs are available to close it. Another hole can then be made nearby. The plugs can also be used when you want to remove a particular dripper completely.

The use of in-line filters will reduce blockage of the drippers. It is essential to use a high quality soluble nutrient preparation and it is advisable in most systems to insert a filter to treat the nutrient solution before it returns to the reservoir. These measures also prolong the life of the electric pump.

It would be counter-productive to give precise instructions and measurements on the setting up of a small recycling system using a specific submersible electric pump and particular types of containers. It is far better for you to find out what is

available locally and build from that. When you have set it up, all you need to do is raise the nutrient solution up to the hydroponic garden and then let it drain back by gravity to its starting point.

There are some additional comments on setting up small systems in Chapter 9 and the author's major system is described in the Epilogue.

Other Hydroponic Systems
Nutrient Film Techniques

These do not use a support medium. The plants are grown in channels, often made by folding black polythene into sloping 'V'-shaped guttering which continuously circulates the nutrient solution past their roots. If one proposes to circulate

HYDROHINT
Here is a Hydrohint which might save your life and others — have an electrician install safety switches.

nutrient either in very small bursts or continuously then lots of fun can be had using this method.

Increasingly, nutrient film techniques are proving a most successful method, not only for commercial growers but also for many amateurs. Labour costs are minimal because dripper blockage does not occur and positioning the plants and harvesting them is extremely easy. The only problem may be a blockage of the channel outlets by the sometimes profuse growth of roots.

There are attractive reasonably-priced kits available which work well and certainly eliminate the need to stoop when one is gardening! Remember that, although drippers aren't needed for this technique, good filtration is required on the returning nutrient solution to remove root debris, etc.

Dry Feeding System

It is possible merely to sprinkle dried nutrient powder on the surface of the medium and water it in instead of preparing a nutrient solution. Some

NUTRIENT FILM TECHNIQUES

<u>A</u> Eggplant showing roots.

<u>B</u> Endives, lettuces and primulas.

<u>C</u> Tomatoes.

commercial growers have used this procedure successfully and in experienced hands it works well, but there are obviously potential problems. For example, a variable concentration may hit the root system when the nutrients are being 'watered in'. In most cases it is also necessary to add water between feeds with the dry nutrient, and the nutrient mixture has to be well mixed to avoid spots of mineral unbalance.

Aeroponics

This takes the nutrient film technique a step further. The roots of the plants are allowed to project into an environment in which they are continually misted with a mixture of air and nutrient solution. This procedure is used in some commercial establishments but it is neither practical nor advantageous to the amateur.

Foliar Feeding

If the leaves of plants are misted with a dilute nutrient solution, they will rapidly absorb it and plant growth can be quite spectacular. Pale yellow nitrogen-deficient plants receiving appropriate foliar feeding will revert to a satisfactory green colour within twelve hours. On the other hand, problems can rapidly develop if the solution is too strong or too weak. Although foliar feeding needs extra time and equipment it is certainly worth considering, even if only as an adjunct to another hydroponic system. Foliar feeding is generally reserved for plants older than four weeks and it should not be done in direct hot sunshine.

In my hydroponic unit, I can spray the foliage of selected plants using a hose and fine rose attached to the circulating system. Since half-strength nutrient solution is used at all times, I merely have to open a valve.

Growth of young plants can be encouraged by regular foliar spraying. When combined with artificial lighting the results can be excellent (see the photograph).

Apart from producing impressive results, such a system can be an attractive centre of interest in a hydroponic system.

A simple aeroponic system available from One Stop Sprinklers.

Liquid Culture or Floating Hydroponics

Professor Gericke (pages xvi–xvii) grew his famous giant tomato plants using liquid culture. The plant is floated over the nutrient solution and the roots dangle down and fan out into the solution. The original technique involved pumps to saturate the solution with air and, because it was rather complicated, it had minimal commercial success.

Nowadays a number of enthusiasts have become keen on liquid culture and I must admit, having dabbled in it, that it is most interesting and good fun. Originally the gardener had to use timber as floats for plants but now there are very cheap and highly buoyant foam plastics available and they prove ideal (see the picture on page 48). The plastic raft is floated several centimetres above the surface of the nutrient solution on a couple of narrow slabs of foam plastic and the plant is carefully inserted into a hole cut in the raft. The tips of the roots are allowed to dangle in the solution into which they soon spread. The roots that are exposed to air absorb oxygen but don't dry out because of the humidity around them. Some people aerate the solution using an aquarium pump.

Light should be prevented from reaching the solution by covering any gaps around the edges of the foam plastic with strips of black plastic sheeting. If this is done, the solution only needs replacing about every four weeks. It is possible to circulate

Foliar feeding: a large stainless steel container holds a variety of plants growing in either perlite/vermiculite mixtures or growool.
During the day, every half an hour, they are automatically misted with half-strength nutrient solution which drains back to the reservoir.
It is pretty to watch and the plants love it. It's a grand way to bring on plants when they are over four weeks old.

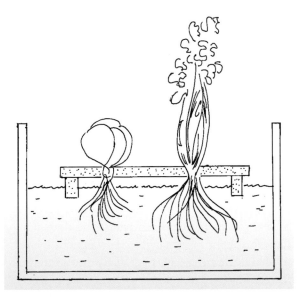

Liquid culture (no medium is used). The plants are floating on a polystyrene raft and part of the roots are exposed to air, the rest extend deep into the nutrient solution.

LIQUID CULTURE

<u>A</u> Display of the root system encouraged by floating hydroponics.

<u>B</u> Root system and details of the raft which supports the plant.

<u>C</u> Celery and lettuce grown by floating hydroponics.

nutrient solution through a series of these little units and this is done very successfully by Mr Geoff Wilson of Melbourne.

Celery and lettuces seem to do very well in this floating system.

For ease of operation my floating hydroponics are connected up to the circulating nutrient solution in the main unit, which increases aeration and keeps the nutrient levels more constant.

Hydroponic Terrariums

A combination of the principle behind terrariums and hydroponic feeding can produce some impressive results. Some manufacturers add artificial lighting to develop units which will grow flowering plants, vegetables and other types of plants indoors all the year around. Such a unit is manufactured by Grotron of Melbourne.

What System Should One Use?

If starting from scratch, I would advise you to operate on a very small scale until you have decided exactly what and how much is to be grown. Visit every hydroponic supplier within range and make contact with a hydroponic society.

In the meantime, especially if it's late spring, start up a few tomato plants in buckets and some lettuces in trays (Chapter 6), using the most accessible medium and nutrient. Perhaps also start a vertical strawberry tube (Chapter 6) if you have a handy spot to hang one. Some chive seeds planted as described in Chapter 6 can give the beginner very impressive results. Let your hydroponics grow like Topsy if you find it rewarding.

Purchasing Hydroponic Kits

There are advantages in buying a hydroponics kit so new-found skills and knowledge can be put into immediate effect. Some well designed and proven

kits are available, which may be cheaper in the long run than building and improvising from scratch. Unfortunately, there are also some which cannot be said to be either of good value and/or good design. The following is a suggested approach.

1 After you've decided on the area where you would like to set up hydroponics, see if there is a display of hydroponic equipment anywhere near your home.
2 Preferably examine the unit (or units) when it is fully functional and seek advice on the suitability of its use in your planned position, and especially its suitability for whatever you want to grow, e.g. herbs, tomatoes, flowers, etc.
3 Check that the unit comes with good instructions and a suitable guarantee, and that spare parts are available. It may even be worthwhile contacting the head office of the firm to obtain catalogues of other products and details of new developments.
4 Check price and ongoing availability of the recommended nutrient solution.

The Appendix lists hydroponics suppliers and displays of equipment are now becoming a routine sight at garden shows, etc. Hydroponics societies are also listed in the Appendix and their members may be a source of sound and ongoing advice.

Chapter 9 contains descriptions of some easy ventures into hydroponics which may help you get started.

You may decide to stick to small-scale hydroponics, using a simple system and recycling by hand, or graduate to the stage when you can appreciate and make valuable use of a submersible pump. Perhaps you may then decide to buy a domestic hydroponic kit or build your own system. By now you will be a dedicated believer in hydroponics and may even contemplate building a small glasshouse or polyhouse. When you become as serious as this, you will have jointed the horticultural elite!

CHAPTER 5

Germinating Seeds and Planting Out

Advantages in Starting from Seed

Seeds are usually free from pests and disease and, by raising one's own babies, healthy vigorous plants which 'take off' with great enthusiasm can be introduced into the hydroponic system. On the other hand, some specimens sold by nurseries may be quite elderly, having had their growth restrained in a crowded and cramped container over many weeks. During this period they may also have come in contact with pests or diseases. A lot of money can be saved by raising plants at home and, at the same time, careful planning guarantees a regular stream of seedlings available to replace plants that are due for removal.

Most nursery plants are raised in earth-containing mixtures which must be removed. How to do this is discussed later, since often the hydroponicer cannot raise all the plants needed.

Information regarding the methods to be used for sowing and cultivating individual vegetables and flowers is given in Chapter 6.

Methods of Germinating Seeds

Direct Sowing

In warmer weather some seeds can be sown directly into a hydroponic system. Perlite is quite a satisfactory medium for growing seeds. Sprinkle them on the surface and then cover them with an additional thin layer of perlite. Some enthusiasts have adopted a routine of sowing a few lettuce seeds in a little cluster in one section of the hydroponic system every fortnight so that a constant supply of small lettuces is available for transplanting. Hardy plants, like most bulbs and cloves of

garlic, can be confidently planted without prior conditioning and the successful raising of chives sown directly into a hydroponic system is described in the Epilogue.

Generally, however, it is better to raise seeds separately, because one can then select only the best seedlings for transplanting. Also, normal nutrient solution may be too strong for some germinating seeds.

Use of Containers

Shallow, well drained plastic or wooden trays are the usual containers for seedlings raised in nurseries. They are shallow to restrict the extension of roots as well as for reasons of economy and weight. Little plastic trays are often used by the home gardener, but they have the disadvantage that the roots of the seedlings become entangled, which leads to damage when they have to be separated.

Foam plastic trays with multiple wedge-shaped compartments are available for raising plants (see the photograph on page 51). The trays are made with large or small compartments, the former being used extensively by commercial tomato growers. The trays are easily subdivided with a sharp knife so that they can be fitted into a germination incubator (see later) and they ensure impressive results for both the hydroponic and conventional gardener. The roots of the seedlings develop in a compact wedge shape and, prior to planting, the plant can be eased out with a table knife. It can then be gently pushed directly into the hydroponic medium or into the garden. Because the root mass is not disturbed by the procedure no 'root or transport shock' develops.

WEDGE-SHAPED COMPARTMENTS FOR SEEDLINGS

<u>A</u> Dwarf dahlia seedlings growing in wedge-shaped compartments (see also silver beet in wedges, Chapter 7).

<u>B</u> Thinning eggplant seedlings: two seeds have germinated in each compartment and scissors are used to cut the smaller off at ground level.

Growool cubes and blocks being used for the commercial production of carnation plants. The cuttings were started in small growool cubes and then 'potted up' into the larger wrapped cubes. (*Courtesy Rick Donnan*)

Even on a hot day planting into the soil can be carried out without loss. For some years I have had great success raising sweet corn seeds in these trays and have planted them into the garden without ever losing a plant. Their light weight makes them ideal for use in the homemade germination incubator.

Unfortunately, these trays are sold in large commercial packs, but with a little hunting around one can usually find a retailer who will sell single trays. They are reuseable and with care will last for many years.

Use of Growool Propagation Blocks

This is a very neat and convenient method, which uses specially cut growool blocks and cubes (see Chapter 3). The seed germinates on a small block of growool (see the photograph) which is later dropped into a hole in a larger cube of growool held together by a plastic wrapper. When the plant has grown, this cube in turn is placed on a large growool slab or in some other hydroponic medium. This clever system never disturbs the roots of the plant and is justifiably becoming very popular. Try

CUTTINGS IN THE HYDROPONIC SYSTEM

A Frangipani struck from a battered branch found on the footpath near the publisher's office. It was cut into sections, dusted lightly with rooting powder and then sprouted with vigour about eight weeks after planting in perlite/vermiculite mixture.

B Hydrangea cuttings striking in a perlite/vermiculite mixture. The ends were dipped in a plant cutting powder before insertion. A neighbour's house had been demolished and its lovely old-fashioned garden scraped away. A remnant of a beautiful hydrangea that was left was the source of these cuttings.

planting two seeds in each block, then cutting off the weakest one after germination.

The propagation blocks must be used with the uncut surface uppermost. The air gaps on the undersurface not only partially divide the block to aid later separation but discourage the roots from extending out of their individual block. Before planting seeds or inserting cuttings, the propagation block should be soaked in water and one-half strength nutrient solution (see pages 20–2). As the wet blocks must be handled carefully to prevent them from coming apart, they are best kept on the same flat surface all the time. The seed should be barely inserted into the upper surface of each cube otherwise it may stay too moist.

I often raise my seedlings using these propagation blocks and sometimes bypass the wrapped cube stage and put the plant directly into the hydroponic system.

Seed-germinating Mixtures

Ideally no earth should be used in the container. A 70/30 mixture of vermiculite and fine grade perlite is recommended. Granulated growool is quite good provided it is only lightly packed into the container.

In practice many hydroponicers use a high grade commercial seed-germinating mixture which does not contain earth and which has been sterilised. These mixtures are available from most nurseries. If a good quality product is used in one of the plastic wedges described on page 50, and the root system is not damaged or disturbed when the plant is removed to the hydroponic system, then the results will be excellent. Seed-germinating mixtures usually contain little or no nutrients and so feeding with one-quarter strength nutrient solution should commence when the seeds germinate.

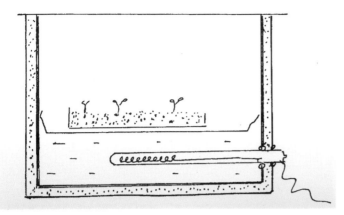

A simple incubator for seed germination.

Importance of Moisture

Germination may cease if the seed's environment is allowed to dry out. The surroundings of the seed must be kept well watered and the drainage must be excellent.

Provided drainage is excellent you cannot overfeed or over-water seedlings.

A Simple Incubator for Germination

The simplest of all ways to assist germination is to place the dampened seed box in a plastic bag which is inflated and then sealed with a rubber band. If kept out of direct sunlight this creates a good moist mini-environment for seed germination. As soon as the seedlings have appeared the bag should be removed.

Seeds germinate much faster if maintained at optimum temperature (see Table 6) in a

Table 6 OPTIMUM TEMPERATURES FOR GERMINATION OF SEEDS

CROP	OPTIMUM (°C)	OPTIMUM (°F)	RANGE °C (MIN. TO MAX.)	RANGE °F (MIN. TO MAX.)
Beans: broad	15	59	5–30	41–86
Beans: French climbing and French dwarf	24	75	15–35	59–95
Beet: red and silver	30	86	5–35	41–95
Brassicas (excl. cauliflower)	30	86	5–35	41–95
Capsicum	30	86	15–35	59–95
Carrot	30	86	15–35	59–95
Cauliflower	27	81	5–35	41–95
Celery	21	70	5–30	41–86
Cucumber	24	75	15–35	59–95
Eggplant	30	86	15–35	54–95
Endive and lettuce	24	75	2–30	36–86
Melons	35	95	15–40	59–104
Onions	27	81	2–35	36–95
Parsley	25	77	5–32	41–90
Parsnip	21	70	2–30	36–86
Peas	24	75	5–30	41–86
Pumpkins and squash	35	95	15–38	59–95
Radish	30	86	5–35	41–95
Spinach	21	70	2–30	36–86
Swedes and turnips	30	86	5–40	41–104
Sweet corn	30	86	10–40	50–104
Tomatoes	24	75	10–35	50–95

This table is reproduced with permission from *Vegetables for Small Gardens and Containers in Australia* by Peter de Vaus, Hyland House, 1982.

germination or propagation incubator. These are fairly expensive to buy, but a simple box can be made using a foam plastic esky (see the picture).

A small, fully submersible aquarium heater set at, say, 25°C (77°F) is placed on the floor of the esky and then covered with at least 8 cm (3 1/6 in) of water. A sheet of plastic is placed on the surface of the water, making a suitable waterbed for the containers to sit on. If a fully submersible heater is not available, a partially submersible one can be used by pushing it through a hole near the bottom of the esky and sealing the hole with silicone sealant. A lid should be placed over the germination incubator so that germination can take place in near darkness. Care must be taken that the heater is always well covered with water, otherwise it may melt the foam plastic.

An electric kitchen frypan provided you have an old one available also works quite well. Set it on its lowest setting.

If using a seed incubator, check the 'hatching rate' every day! If germinated plants are left in too long, spectacular but spindly growth may occur.

> **HYDROHINT**
> Raising seeds in single compartments allows easier transplantation.

> **HYDROHINT**
> A wide range of simple incubators and heated mats are available for seed germination.

Seeds germinate at variable rates and you should inspect the germination incubator daily. When the baby seedlings appear they must be moved out into an environment which has light as well as warmth. If the batch of seedlings are all at the same stage, then they can be left in the incubator and the lid replaced with clear glass, leaving an adequate gap for ventilation. Alternatively, you can use a light producing artificial sunlight to stimulate rapid growth (see Chapter 7).

Some seeds like cucumber and broccoli germinate at breakneck speed and usually require only a day or so in the germination incubator. Others ruminate for perhaps a week before they decide to get their act together. Information on the seed packet usually gives a fair idea of relative germination rates and it is advisable to put seeds with a similar germination rate in the same container.

Introducing Seedlings and Plants to the System

Seedlings you have grown yourself probably offer no problems, as they should be healthy and have their roots in an organised block or wedge so that they can go straight into or onto the medium. If a seed-germinating mixture containing soil (see above) has been used, the root system should be gently washed in fresh water.

Some hydroponic mediums like scoria are quite abrasive so the site of planting should first be excavated then the medium gently replaced around the plant. For information on transplanting seedlings grown in growool, see pages 20–1.

If you are using seedlings from a nursery which are in a soil-filled punnet then great care must be

TOMATOES

A This tomato was grown in a seed-raising mixture. Most of the soil has been carefully washed away under a running tap, exposing the delicate root system. It is about to be inserted into well washed granulated growool.

B The same tomato seen three weeks later.

taken in their preparation. As much soil as possible must be washed away from the roots and, of course, the plants must be separated from each other. One cannot overstress the importance of tender treatment at this stage, as any roughness will result in damage to the root system and poor growth or even death on transplanting. Ideally, the punnet containing the plants should be soaked for three or four hours in water and then the plant's root system washed and separated using a gentle stream of water. It is not a bad idea to repeat this several times in order to have a clean root network. Some people recommend that the roots be washed in a weak antifungal solution such as Benlate.

After preparation the plants can be gently placed in the medium. No matter how careful one has been there will be damage to the root hairs so the plants will have difficulty in absorbing nutrient solution when placed in their permanent sites.

HYDROHINT
After moving them, protect plants from intense heat and dehydration.

Cherish your seedlings.

Give spare seedlings to neighbours, or overcrowding will lead to disease and poor crops.

Therefore, it is very important that they be protected from intense heat and dehydration. Ideally, they should be kept from direct sunlight for a day or so after transplanting.

Usually you can commence feeding nutrient solution immediately after planting. See Chapter 9 for advice on some specific plants.

If you have planted purchased plants in the holes of hydrotubes (see Chapter 4) then, apart from taking special pains to avoid root damage, it is advisable to keep the whole system in a cool place for several days while the root hairs re-establish themselves. A bathroom is often a good place. You should also run water through the hydrotube from time to time.

Sources of Seeds and Plants

Unfortunately, the quality of seeds, especially in regard to percentage germination rate, varies from one manufacturer to another and from year to year. A good reliable source is essential and once found it pays to report any failures immediately. There are a number of very good seed firms which distribute informative mail-order catalogues, often including many less common seed types (see Appendix).

Fortunately, there are producers of plants, such as strawberries and carnations, who sell stock that is guaranteed free from certain diseases. Many nurseries act as outlets for viral-free strawberry plants, but pathogen-free carnations are more difficult to find. A direct order service is available from Mr Bagulay (see Appendix).

> **HYDROHINT**
> Transfer plants very gently. Pretend you're a plastic surgeon doing a skin graft. If it's done gently the plant should hardly be aware that it's been upped and moved.

Swapping of Seedlings

Few gardeners care to discard any excess plants they have raised; it is like murdering one's own children. It is a very good idea to develop a swap system with other enthusiasts as this gives you more experience with different types of plants. The keen hydroponicer will always find room to try a new plant in the system provided it is young and healthy.

If the worse comes to the worst, plants can always be given away to those poor wretches who are still gardening the old-fashioned way with mud, weeds and slugs. Perhaps do them a favour and introduce them to seedlings grown in wedges or growool.

> **HYDROHINT**
> Check that the seeds are not time expired.

Sharing of Seeds

Many seeds are wasted because they become time expired. It would be interesting to know how many seeds are discarded when it is noticed that the 'plant before' date is some four or five years old! I lend my seed collection to friends each spring and this reduces waste and further strengthens the bonds between fellow hydroponicers.

CHAPTER 6

What to Grow

If by law the amateur was allowed to grow only ten types of plant hydroponically, then I could happily survive because I have ten favourites. The vegetables are beans (French beans), lettuces, tomatoes; my herbs would be chives, mint, parsley and thyme; then would come strawberries; and the flowers would be carnations and roses. Everyone has their own favourite ten but I will bet at least three of the above will be found on almost everyone's list.

Choice of Mediums and Containers

Most plants will do well in any medium and, because in hydroponics a well fed root system does not have to be as extensive as in conventional gardening, the medium usually only has to be 10 to 20 cm (4 to 8 in) deep, depending upon the anticipated mature plant size. Accordingly, in the majority of cases one can use any type of container and any commercial medium. In some cases certain mediums suit the crop better and these are specifically mentioned in dealing with individual plants below. Sometimes both a specific medium and a deep container are required. Carrots are a classic example, where a depth of 20 cm (8 in) of perlite is needed to allow adequate growth combined with ease of harvesting. Some plants have been shown to produce maximum yields in specially designed containers. The best example of this is found with strawberries growing in the vertical plastic strawberry bag described in this chapter.

Grow your own delicious Asian vegetables.

Amaranth spinach (Een Choi) growing very well in a perlite/vermiculite mixture.

Vegetables

Let us now consider some vegetables alphabetically, indicating which are the most suitable for growing hydroponically. Of course there is always room for experimentation and if you want to try any plant hydroponically, then go for it. Some additional notes and observations on plant selection and results can be found in Chapter 9 and the Epilogue.

Amaranth Spinach (Een Choi)

This Chinese vegetable grows very well in a perlite/vermiculite mixture. It has attractive red tinges to its leaves. The whole plant can be harvested or the tips of the larger plants taken off as required.

Artichokes (Globe or Jerusalem)

These grow very well in perlite and are especially tender.

Asparagus

Asparagus requires a couple of years before it produces a reasonable harvest and, in the meantime, occupies space and needs a bed at least 25 cm (10 in) deep. However, I have grown it successfully in plastic buckets with perlite as the medium (see Epilogue).

French beans growing in a length of drainage pipe which has been packed with granulated growool up to 30 cm (12 in) from the holes. Seeds are dropped into the holes and germinate on the medium. This pipe has been in continuous use for three years with no medium change.

Asparagus growing in perlite in an old wooden laundry trough. The perlite is 30 cm (12 in) deep.

Table 7 SELECTION OF PLANTS, MEDIUMS AND CONTAINERS

Note: Only some of the more common plants are considered in this table. Most plants thrive under the correct hydroponic conditions so don't hesitate to experiment with plants not mentioned if they appeal to you.

PLANT	HYDROPONIC RESULTS	RECOMMENDED MEDIUM AND MINIMUM DEPTH*
Artichokes globe and Jerusalem	good	Perlite, 25 cm (10 in)
Asparagus	good	Perlite, 25 cm (10 in)
Aubergine (eggplant)	excellent	Any medium, 10 cm (4 in)
Bananas	good	Perlite, scoria, 40 cm (16 in)
Basil	excellent	Any medium, 10 cm (4 in)
Beans (broad)	excellent	Any medium, 15 cm (6 in)
Beans (French)	excellent	Any medium, 10 cm (4 in)
Beetroot	excellent	Any medium, 10 cm (4 in)
Broccoli	excellent	Any medium, 10 cm (4 in)
Brussels sprouts	good	Any medium, 10 cm (4 in)
Cabbage	excellent	Any medium, 10 cm (4 in)
Capsicum	excellent	Any medium, 10 cm (4 in)
Carnations (Sim)	excellent	Growool slabs or perlite, 8 cm (3 in)
Carrots	excellent	Perlite, 15–30 cm (6–12 in) deep depending upon type of carrot
Cauliflowers	excellent	Any medium, 10 cm (4 in)
Celery	good	Any medium, 10 cm (4 in)
Chives	excellent	Any medium, 8 cm (3 in)
Cucumber	excellent	Any medium, 8–15 cm (3–6 in)
Dahlias (miniature)	excellent	Any medium, 10 cm (4 in)
Flowers		All flowers have done well except tuberoses. See Carnations, Dahlias, Roses, Strawflowers and Sweet William.
Garlic	excellent	Any medium, 10 cm (4 in)
Herbs		See Basil, Chives, Garlic, Mint, Parsley and Thyme.
Horseradish	excellent	Perlite, granulated growool, 25 cm (10 in)
Leeks	excellent	Any medium, 10 cm (4 in)
Lettuces	excellent	Any medium, 10 cm (4 in)
Lobelia	excellent	Any medium, 8 cm (3 in)
Marrows (spaghetti)	good	Any medium, 10 cm (4 in)
Marrows (zucchini)	excellent	Any medium, 15 cm (6 in)
Melons	good	Any medium, 10 cm (4 in)
Mint	excellent	Any medium, 10 cm (4 in)
Onions	excellent	Any medium, 10 cm (4 in)
Parsley	excellent	Any medium, 15 cm (6 in)
Parsnips	excellent	Perlite, 25 cm (10 in)
Peas	excellent	Any medium, 10 cm (4 in)
Potatoes	excellent	Perlite, granulated growool, 30 cm (12 in)
Radishes	excellent	Any medium, 10 cm (4 in)
Rhubarb	excellent	Any medium, 15 cm (6 in)
Roses	excellent	Any medium, 20–25 cm (8–10 in)
Silverbeet (Chard)	excellent	Any medium, 10 cm (4 in)
Spinach	excellent	Any medium, 10 cm (4 in)
Strawberries	excellent	Perlite, granulated growool. See strawberry bags, pages 73–8
Strawflowers	excellent	Any medium, 10 cm (4 in)
Sweet corn **	excellent	Any medium, 15 cm (6 in)
Sweet peas	excellent	Any medium, 10 cm (4 in)
Sweet William	excellent	Any medium, 10 cm (4 in)
Thyme	excellent	Any medium, 10 cm (4 in)
Tomatoes	excellent	Any medium, 15 cm (6 in)
Tuberoses	poor	Perlite

* Not relevant to growool slabs.

** There are great advantages in raising sweet corn seeds hydroponically and then planting out the advanced seedlings later in the garden. See page 51.

Aubergine (Eggplant)

Hydroponic aubergine can be quite successful, but the plant thrives with warmth and can only be grown in the summer months in most districts. To grow large fruit each plant should have all but two or three fruit removed just after they have formed.

Beans (Broad Beans)

These are not recommended for hydroponic growth because of the time and space they need.

Beans (French Beans) (highly recommended)

Jack, of Bean Stalk fame, may have used hydroponics. Even in the strange climate of Melbourne, two and perhaps three crops of hydroponic beans can be grown in an unprotected hydroponic system each year. Additional and better crops are obtained in a glasshouse or igloo. The most popular are the dwarf stringless beans. Nothing seems to stop the rapid growth of beans provided feeding is adequate and the important good drainage maintained.

Seeds can be sown into the growing medium. If using perlite the seeds should be covered so that they are just out of sight. With growool care must be taken that the seeds are not planted too deeply, otherwise they may rot. If they are just one-quarter buried in growool and a sheet of paper placed over them to protect them from direct sunlight for the first week, they grow very well.

It is important to pick the beans while they are young and fresh and replace the plants as soon as possible. Do not let them linger on for a month or so after their peak output. Harvest them regularly to encourage them to crop for a longer period.

Climbing beans do very well in hydroponics but take care that they do not hog the sunlight and grow them at the rear of the shorter plants. Make sure, too, that you provide a secure framework about 1.5 metres (4 ft 11 in) high to support them as they climb.

Beans are ideal for snap freezing.
See also Epilogue.

Beetroot growing in perlite.

Beetroot

Beetroots do well hydroponically and one avoids a lot of weeding. One advantage is that they require only moderate light and need little attention. However, by the time they have matured and taken up space for a long while the shops are usually filled with good quality cheap beet. On the other hand, if you wish to grow them out of season this can be done hydroponically provided the environment is sufficiently warm and well lit.

See also Epilogue.

Brassicas: Broccoli, Brussels Sprouts, Cabbages and Cauliflowers

The experts have no problems growing these staple items hydroponically but the amateur is often disappointed. Some grow very slowly and take up much valuable space. Broccoli is perhaps the most rewarding (see Epilogue). Try to obtain broccoli seeds of different varieties so you can harvest over a longer time. Skiff and

HYDROHINT
Usually a vermiculite/perlite mixture produces better results than perlite alone. Even a couple of handfuls of vermiculite mixed into the top 8 cm (3 in) of the perlite helps the young plants establish themselves.

Calabrese are a good combination. Brussels sprouts needs frosty weather so can be grown in a cold climate. Cabbage can be grown all the year round like lettuce. Choose mini cauliflowers which take up less space.

Capsicum

These thrive under hydroponic conditions just like tomatoes. At least one plant should be grown each year, but allow plenty of space as it does not like being crowded in by other plants. A plant that is pruned back in winter may last two seasons.

See also Chapter 9 and Epilogue.

Carrots

If you have the space and some deep containers, growing carrots is good fun. Perlite is the perfect medium and the seeds should be sparingly sprinkled on the surface. Be careful you don't let them dry out. I thin the maturing carrots and hand them to visitors who, to date, have always munched them there and then. Basically, I grow only the smaller carrots mainly for salads and buy the larger cooking types. It all depends on the amount of space you have.

See also Chapter 9.

A Young broccoli and basil plants growing in a growool slab which is covered with opaque plastic.

Celery

Celery is a challenge to the amateur and few succeed in producing the classic tall blanched end product. On the brighter side, celery leaves give a delightful flavour to most dishes and even the most misshapen celery plant can provide a regular source of suitable leaves.

If you want to try to blanch your celery, you must keep the stems away from the light for one month before harvest. This can be done by wrapping the stems in opaque white plastic sheeting or newspaper.

See also Epilogue.

B Hydroponic broccoli ready for harvest.

Chinese Soup Celery (see Kintsai)

Cucumber (highly recommended)

Dr Johnson expressed the view that cucumbers should be well sliced, dressed with pepper and vinegar and then thrown out as good for nothing. I also dislike cucumbers, perhaps even more intensely, but growing them hydroponically is irresistible because of their phenomenal growth rate when adequately supplied with water and nutrients.

Cucumbers require constant attention in order to guide their growth up an appropriate trellis, otherwise they run mad and fruit develop in the most inaccessible corners. So keep a close eye on this plant and limit it to a predetermined region. Remove any deformed, i.e. curling cucumbers, and always pick them before they become huge and coarse. This will also frustrate their habit of crashing down on more delicate plants or upon visitors. The burpless and mildew-resistant types are very popular.

Cucumber seeds germinate almost overnight if raised in a germination incubator (Chapter 5).

Above right: Capsicum growing in a plastic laundry bucket filled with perlite.

Right: Cucumbers arising from small slabs of growool reach almost to the roof of the igloo if given a trellis to climb. The more you pick them the faster they seem to grow.

Far right: Kintsai, Chinese soup celery.

<u>Right:</u> Leeks growing in narrow troughs filled with perlite.

<u>Far right:</u> Lettuces growing in perlite with young leeks in the background.

Transplant them immediately into the hydroponic system. They do well in any type of medium. If left for a day or so longer in the incubator, they grow into pale plants 10 or 15 cm (4 or 6 in) in length which are not suitable for transferring anywhere.

Kintsai (Chinese Soup Celery)

This grows very well in a perlite/vermiculite mixture and leaves can be regularly removed six weeks after germination. It has a beautiful aroma and when cooked the leaves stay a vivid green.

Leeks

These grow at a slow but steady rate under hydroponic conditions and it is useful to have them constantly available for special dishes. I grew them in troughs alternately with strawberries before I started using the strawberry bags (page 73), and the two types of plants make an attractive combination. Leeks are admirable if one wants a long-term display of one's hydroponic prowess.

The seeds can be sown directly onto perlite in the germination incubator.

See also Epilogue.

Lettuces (highly recommended)

Herbs aside, there is no stronger reason for getting into home hydroponics than the production of lettuces. The systemic raising of hydroponic lettuces is probably a sound economic proposition for most families. The seeds germinate well and can be ready for planting within a short time. It takes a few seconds each fortnight to sow another three or four seeds to ensure a constant supply of mature plants over a four to five month period. Most people sprinkle the seeds in a clump in perlite beside established plants and transplant them as required.

Fast grown lettuces are almost disease-free and there is little or no waste with a hydroponic lettuce. Good drainage is essential for maximum growth and any aged leaves around the base of the plant should be removed, both to keep the plant healthy and for the sake of appearance. If grown in their own individual growool slabs the plants can be shuffled around to positions within the system to suit their need for sunlight. However, growing lettuces in summer is more successful if they are well shaded. They only need about five hours of sunshine a day and they are very sensitive to excessive heat.

When ready, the intact plant on its growool slab can be brought into the kitchen where the outer leaves can be removed for salad and the plant then replaced. Thus you needn't sacrifice the whole plant for a salad and can make use of its ability to go on growing. If you want to pick the whole lettuce, you can store it in the refrigerator for two to three weeks, which is in contrast to the three or four day survival of most lettuces purchased in a shop.

One popular lettuce is the Mignonette variety which may be grown the whole year round as long as heating is provided in midwinter. The more common heart-forming lettuce also does very well in hydroponics and harvesting time is considerably shortened. It is wise to consult your nurseryperson as to the appropriate seeds or plants to use.

Marrows

As with cucumbers, the growth of marrows can be most satisfactory under hydroponic conditions. You must allow several square metres or feet for each plant, particularly for the larger species. If you grow them in an insect-screened igloo, you will have to pollinate by hand because of the exclusion of bees.

An exotic marrow called the spaghetti marrow is a fun plant. After the intact marrow has been boiled for twenty minutes or so and cut open, its flesh can be forked out and has a similar appearance and taste to spaghetti. This interesting marrow must be trained onto a trellis or into one area as it tends to take off in all directions.

Zucchini is very popular and a large yield may be obtained provided the crop is regularly harvested before it reaches the length of, say, 20 cm (8 in).

Melons

Like marrows, melon plants will take over the whole area but, provided they are trained to develop well away from the other hydroponically grown plants, their cultivation is worth considering. Melons require pollination by bees and hand-pollination will be necessary in a glasshouse.

Below: A fine spaghetti marrow.

Bottom: Pak Choi, the white Chinese cabbage.

Onions

Onions are not economic propositions hydroponically unless you have lots of space, since they are usually available at a low price and many other plants are more useful in the hydroponic garden.

Pak Choi White

This Chinese cabbage does splendidly in a hydroponic system. It likes a perlite/vermiculite mixture. Give it plenty of room and harvesting will be possible from six weeks on.

Peas

Although peas grow well in a hydroponic system, the yield for the area they occupy makes them a dubious proposition for the small-scale hydroponicer.

Whereas a row of French beans may give many meals, a similar row of peas produces a relatively unsatisfactory yield. If you have enough room, by all means grow peas, particularly the high-yielding climbing types. The snow pea with a pod that is eaten whole is a good plant to consider.

Potatoes

If sufficient space is available have a go at hydroponic potatoes. For best results, always plant certified seed potatoes rather than spares from the kitchen. Potatoes cannot, of course, be grown in shallow troughs but need large plastic containers which can be incorporated in a recirculating hydroponic system. Laundry buckets as described in Chapter 9 are suitable for this purpose.

A seed potato is placed on 10 cm (4 in) of medium (perlite gives good results) and covered by a further 5 cm (2 in) of medium. The nutrient fluids may be dripped from above to the vicinity of the potato. When the shoots have reached 7.5 cm (3 in) above the medium, they are then covered with further medium. This process is repeated until the top of the bucket is reached and the foliage can then grow quite freely. I often cut the bottom off a second bucket and put it on top of the first to give even more room. When harvest time comes the bucket is disconnected from the hydroponic system and emptied out. It is quite amazing how many new potatoes can pack themselves into a single bucket.

Radishes

At the age of four these were the first seeds I ever grew. I found radishes revolting then and still do; however, they are fine for decoration and they grow well hydroponically. The seeds

have to be sown directly onto the medium because they will not stand the shock of transplantation. Like carrots, it is usually best to grow the short varieties.

Rhubarb

Rhubarb grows well hydroponically and needs plenty of room. The crown should be almost completely covered by the medium. The ripe rhubarb stems should be pulled off the plant and not cut. Care must be taken not to yank the whole plant out of the medium while doing this. Rhubarb grows well in all mediums and as well in deep containers as in growool slabs.

Silver Beet or Chard

This family standby is a very popular hydroponic plant. Tough and easy to grow, it can usually be found in most home hydroponics. Rainbow chard has brightly coloured stems and is both

<u>Left:</u> These potatoes have just been taken out of the igloo for harvesting. One of the double bucket containers is filled with granulated growool, the other with perlite.

<u>Above:</u> Young silverbeet.

Jenny with a giant hydroponic squash plant growing in perlite/vermiculite mixture. This had to go as it threatened to take over the igloo!

attractive and delicious. Because it can be grown the whole year round, silver beet is used by some experts as a monitor for satisfactory hydroponic conditions.

Like rhubarb, the leaves should be harvested by gently tearing off rather that using a knife or scissors. Beet grown on growool slabs can be regularly harvested for twelve months or more.

See also Chapter 9.

Spinach

I have found it far more satisfactory to grow spinach hydroponically than in the garden. The seeds can be sprinkled in rows on perlite in the system and then very lightly covered. In the hot summer months, spinach should be protected from strong sunlight.

Apart from its fast growth, hydroponic spinach has the added advantage that it does not require the onerous and often delicate task of weeding between the small plants.

Squash

Squash grow with great rapidity, sometimes to monstrous size. Good ventilation is essential to reduce incidence of mildew.

Sweet Corn

Plenty of space is required for this plant and so it is not a good candidate for hydroponic culture. It is really very easy to grow in the average garden. Of course, if normal gardening is not possible because of any number of factors, such as shortage of water, then hydroponic sweet corn might be well worth consideration. The advantages of raising sweet corn seedlings hydroponically are described on page 51.

Tomatoes (highly recommended)

Tomatoes are probably the most popular hydroponic crop and the end product is usually far

A harvest of half-hydroponic half-conventional gardening sweet corn.

Young tomato plants growing in perlite-filled laundry buckets. Support is given by winding them round vertical green wires which are attached to the buckets. Lateral growths have been removed.

superior to the specimens sold by fruiterers. Most commercial tomatoes are picked green and the long lasting varieties which are often pale when cut usually taste wooden. A good hydroponic tomato will have a thin bright red skin and fabulously juicy flavoursome interior. I haven't bought a tomato in ten years and often shudder with distaste when passing what are sold to the locals as tomatoes.

Apart from their superior quality, most people find hydroponic tomatoes produce a crop some six to eight weeks ahead of those grown in soil. In milder climates this allows for their use in early summer salads. If a second crop is started in mid-summer, the last tomatoes can be picked five months later.

The most popular types are Grosse Lisse, a large plant with huge fruit, and King-Humbert which bears a prolific egg-shaped crop. Some varieties, like Apollo and Rouge de Mamande, produce fruit through winter. Moonshot and the Heritage tomatoes give impressive results. Miniature tomatoes like Tiny Tim have a strong

following, especially among those who garden on small balconies.

Tomato seedlings are easily raised. Usually two seeds are placed in each block or unit (see Chapter 5) and, if both germinate, the smaller is cut off rather than pulled out so that its partner's root system won't be damaged. By spring you should have six-week-old individually potted plants about 15 cm (6 in) tall which are ideal for transferring to the hydroponic system. My best results have been with tomatoes grown in plastic buckets filled with perlite or granulated growool (see Epilogue).

Support for tomatoes, such as stakes or hanging string, should be in place before planting. I use plastic-coated wire and find it easy to induce the plant to spiral itself up the wire. This is a neat looking support system which allows plenty of air movement. Once growth is accelerating the bottom leaves of the plant should be removed and only two main stems allowed to develop. The stems which sprout near the base of the plant should be pinched out, as otherwise a flat spreading disease-prone growth will occur. This

TAKING THE LATERALS OFF A TOMATO PLANT

<u>A</u> Three laterals which should be removed are clearly seen in this photograph.

<u>B</u> The laterals have now been nipped off. They often regrow so check the plants every week or so.

unwanted growth often stealthily reappears a few weeks later so check the plants regularly. When your tomatoes are growing vigorously the side shoots or laterals must be removed, usually every week. Generally the side shoots alternate with the flower-bearing growth which one does not want to remove. The earlier these side shoots are pinched or snapped off the better. Pollination will be helped by giving the flowering plants a gentle shake several times a week and hosing down gently and regularly.

As the plant grows, thin out excess fruit and foliage. This is very hard for the beginner to do but, if misshapen fruit is removed and tomatoes limited to two or three per cluster, the total harvest and its quality will be much better.

Adequate access to water and nutrients must be provided to satisfy these fast-growing plants. Inadequate watering will lead to the cracking of fruit. With a little care, beginners will be picking tomatoes 10 cm (4 in) or more in diameter in their first season.

See also Chapter 9.

Herbs (highly recommended)

Herbs are ideal for hydroponics, being generally compact high-yielding plants of great culinary value. See Chapter 9 for instructions on a small herb garden. Of the many herbs available, the following five are the most popular.

Chives (see also Epilogue)

A generous sprinkling of seeds directly onto perlite or growool will produce a lush crop some 15 cm (6 in) high in less than two months. The seeds should be lightly covered with paper or kept in the shade until you can see the shoots. Chives can be progressively cut back to 2 cm (3/4 in) of the surface of the medium again and again to provide a non-stop supply. Do this by starting at one end and moving steadily along in stages over several weeks. By the time you get to the end the first cut chives will be 10 or more centimetres (4 in) high and ready for harvesting again. The more they are harvested the happier

CHIVES GROWING ON GROWOOL BLOCKS

A Young chives germinating on the surface of growool blocks.

B The same chives five weeks later. They can now be regularly cut back.

and healthier they will be. If not chopped back regularly, they become coarse and produce pretty blue flowers. Diseases such as black aphids may also attack them at base level. Chive plants are very easy to divide and transplant. They also thrive and look very attractive in hydrotubes (pages 39–41).

If chives are grown on a series of small blocks of growool, these can successively be brought into the kitchen and then later returned to the system. Not having to sort the weeds out of hydroponic chives is a wonderful time saver.

See also Epilogue.

Garlic

Push the outer cloves halfway into the medium and, if they are healthy and undamaged, when next you look at them they will have sprouted 30 cm (12 in) or so high! When mature and ready for lifting the leaves will turn yellow.

See also Epilogue.

Mint

Mint is easy to grow from root-bearing cuttings in any medium in any type of container. Unless care is taken, the roots will sneakily extend right through the medium and shoots will pop up everywhere, so mint is best grown in growool blocks which can be periodically lifted for the removal of adventurous roots. It should be regularly cut back in stages.

Keep a close eye on mint for insect pests.

I have also grown mint successfully in hydrotubes, possibly because the other herbs have grown vigorously in their allotted spaces. I regard this as an uncharacteristic respect for territorial boundaries.

Parsley

Parsley is a must to grow, since it is superb for both flavouring and decorating food. Seeds can be raised directly in the medium but most people find their very slow and often unsuccessful germination to be frustrating and prefer to start them in the

Right: Garlic growing on a growool slab.

Far right: A laundry bucket filled with granulated growool is obviously a good home for mint.

Below right: Thyme.

germination incubator.

Seedlings do well even in relatively shallow growool blocks. They look good and thrive if sharing a plastic bucket with other larger plants like tomatoes. In hydrotubes they should be the topmost herb planted to allow for their long root development.

Thyme

Thyme is a quiet little plant which goes about its business unobtrusively in a hydroponic garden. It likes as much sunlight as possible, so check regularly that it is not being shaded by other faster-growing plants, and it thrives on the sunniest aspect of a hydrotube. I tend to plonk thyme cuttings or seeds at random throughout the hydroponic system as the little plants are useful gifts and take up little space.

THESE HERBS CAN ALSO BE GROWN SUCCESSFULLY IN A HYDROPONIC SYSTEM:

basil (two types), catmint, dill, marjoram, oregano, sage and tarragon. It is worth trying out other herbs that you particularly like for your cooking as most will do well.

A Basil, green ruffles.

B Basil, sweet.

C Catmint.

D Dill.

E Rosemary.

F Sweet marjoram.

G Oregano.

H Sage.

Strawberries (very highly recommended)

The myth that hydroponic strawberries are watery and tasteless evaporates when the first plump strawberry is devoured. Not only are they juicy and flavoursome, but they are of a delightfully smooth texture, since they lack the hard pithy core often present in those grown slowly on the ground.

So useful is a regular harvest of fine strawberries that it is worth the extra effort to create the ideal conditions for their hydroponic growth. Provided drainage is very good, strawberries thrive in troughs and trays. However, the use of a vertical strawberry bag or tube allows highly concentrated plant growing as well as accessibility for the almost routine evening delight of strawberry picking and is a must for most enthusiasts.

Vertical Strawberry Bag or Tube (see the pictures)

This container is usually made out of a length of black polythene sausage which is narrowed below to prevent loss of the medium but allow drainage. Although it is possible quickly to 'knock up' a simple arrangement with little framework, as in the roughly made strawberry bag (see picture on the left), in most cases the end result will be a disaster with medium and/or plants suddenly falling out onto the ground. A carefully constructed unit is so useful and rewarding that it's worth taking an hour or so to make it properly after spending a few dollars on the components.

The biggest problem with strawberry bags is that of weight. Care must be taken that their overall volume is not too large otherwise, when packed with medium which has absorbed water, the weight may be too great to suspend comfortably. A reasonable size is one with a length of some 60 cm (24 in) and diameter about 20 cm (8 in), as this is sufficient for twenty-four strawberry plants.

A quick way of making a strawberry bag has been popularised by Anne Garton and Fred Funnell. I use the more solid structure described below but, before considering it in detail, a description of this simpler strawberry bag will be

<u>A</u> Strawberries growing on growool.

<u>B</u> Strawberries growing in a perlite/vermiculite mixture.

given. It is called the *two pot strawberry bag*. The bag is made of a section of heavy grade black polythene sausage which, when laid flat, is 32 cm (12 1/2 in) wide. You may have trouble obtaining a short length because it is usually sold in large rolls direct to commercial growers, to be filled with water for use as 'heat banks' in their glasshouses. It is also known as agricultural fluming and is used to transport water across fields, etc., under low pressure. I discussed the difficulty some people were having in buying small lengths of sausage with Fred Funnell of Hydroponic City (see Appendix) and he has undertaken to send suitable lengths to customers anywhere in Australia. Better still, if requested, he will send out a complete 'do-it-yourself' kit with nutrient mix, etc.

Having obtained the heavy grade sausage described above you will also need two plastic plant pots with an upper diameter of 20 cm (8 in).

The first plant pot is pushed firmly into one end of the sausage with the open end at the top and 15 cm (6 in) of the sausage is folded into the plant pot (see the pictures on the right). The second plant pot is lowered into the first with the open end at the top. Make sure the little drainage holes at the bottom of the two plant pots do not lie immediately over each other.

The second plant pot is pushed as far down as possible wedging the folded end of the sausage bag between the two pots. A hot soldering iron or heated screwdriver is then pushed through the upper part of the sausage bag four or five times to weld the pots together. A strong wire loop to hang the bag from can be tied to two of these holes opposite each other.

The bag is then upended and the open end filled with medium as far as the pots. When it is full put a piece of plastic shadecloth on top of the medium to prevent its escape and partially close the end with plastic-coated wire or some other strong material. The bag is now ready to be planted and hung up.

You will have to cut holes in the polythene as you plant the strawberries and will not be able to plant them when you insert the medium as described later. Suspend the bag in the same way as the more solid structure I use.

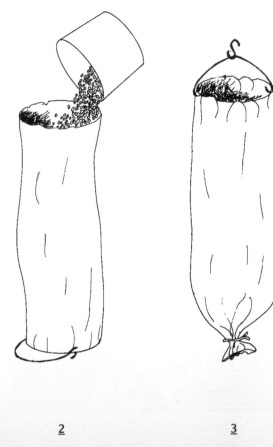

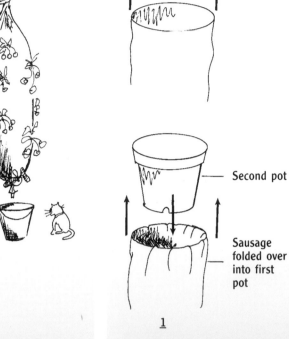

First pot

Second pot

Sausage folded over into first pot

1

2

3

Left: A roughly made strawberry bag—a recipe for trouble.

Right: 1 The two pot strawberry bag (see text). Black plastic sausage is folded over a plastic plant pot and then a second identical plant pot is jammed inside the first one and heat sealed in position.
2 A handle is attached and the bag tipped upside down and filled with medium.
3 After tying the end of the bag (see text) the bag can be suspended the right way up; then it is ready for the insertion of strawberry plants.

A Making a two pot strawberry bag.

B Two strawberry bags (the strawberries in the nearest bag have only been growing there for about ten weeks).

These strawberries are growing in a welded frame. The funnel can be seen sitting neatly in the lower ring of the frame.

A framework for an accident proof strawberry bag.

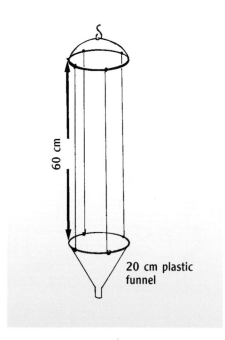

60 cm

20 cm plastic funnel

I prefer a more solidly made strawberry bag for both appearance and function. A bag which has a rigid outer frame can be carefully filled with medium from above as the individual strawberry plants are introduced one at a time. A well-made frame will last for years and is well worth the effort.

The frame is based around a 20 cm (8 in) diameter plastic funnel which acts as the outlet for the nutrient solution. A green funnel looks better than the common bright red one.

If you are a home welder or have access to a welding shop then a good frame can easily be built. Often a tentative request for help from a local garage will lead to a quick welding job done gratis. Upon reflection I have had a lot of welding jobs done and later settled the account with hydroponic tomatoes!

Wrought-iron rods are the best material to use if you can get welding done. These are quite cheap and are stocked by the larger hardware shops. You will need 2 m (6 ft 7 in) of both 10 mm (2/5 in) and 3 mm (1/8 in) rods. The heavier gauge is used to make the upper and lower rings and the 3 mm

material is for the four vertical connecting pieces which can be up to 70 cm (27 1/2 in) long. Incidentally, don't be tempted to make them longer than 70 cm (27 1/2 in) because you will find the total weight of the filled bag to be far too heavy. Once armed with your funnel and the rods ask the welder to make the bottom ring of such a size that the funnel fits comfortably in it but does not drop out. After the bottom ring is constructed the upper ring should be made of similar size and a supporting loop (also of 10 mm (2/5 in) rod) can be welded to it. The four vertical rods can then be welded to the rings at intervals of ninety degrees. You now have a solid and long-lasting frame.

The plastic funnel is dropped into the lower ring to which it is firmly attached by drilling a series of small holes and threading small gauge wire through the holes and around the ring. Plastic-coated garden wire is ideal for this purpose. Next fit black polythene inside the frame. If you are using the black sausage described in the two pot strawberry bag, then it is quite simple to drop a

Strawberry bag using funnel and trellis.

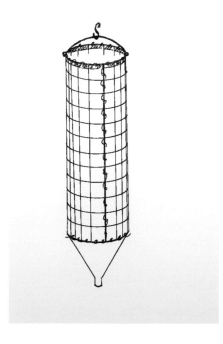

the plastic sheeting can be rolled loosely into a cylinder, pushed into the unit and down into the funnel, and opened up so that it is in contact with the sides. At the top the excess plastic should be folded outwards over the top ring after making a few careful cuts with scissors. As was done with the plastic sausage, some shadecloth can then be pushed into the funnel to retain the medium.

If you cannot get your frame welded, it is still quite easy to make a serviceable unit built around a funnel and trellis. Use the same sized square of trellis as above, roll it into a cylinder and 'sew' it to the funnel with plastic-coated wire, using the same kind of wire to join up the opposing edges of the trellis. Two other steps are required. First, you need something rigid at the top to keep the shape of the unit and also for attaching a handle for suspending the bag. If you cut off the top 5 cm (2 in) of a heavy plastic pot plant this may prove suitable. It can be 'sewn' into the upper opening of the trellis with plastic-coated wire. A handle of heavy gauge wire — at least fencing wire strength — can be inserted into opposite sides through both plastic pot plant and trellis. Second, it's wise to give the trellis some extra support by running four wires or nylon cords from the upper rim down to the funnel.

Obviously many other materials can be used to make a suitable framework for a strawberry bag and once made they should be lined with a plastic sausage or sheeting as described above.

We are now ready to fill the bag with medium and strawberry plants. A bag of the dimensions described will comfortably hold about twenty-four plants.

After the bag has been suspended vertically, dampened perlite can be slowly inserted, compressing and shaping the plastic sheeting against the framework. Granulated growool is another good medium to use. The twenty-four strawberry plants should be introduced at intervals through holes cut in the plastic, starting at the bottom. For each plant, trim the roots, fan them out, and then cover with

HYDROHINTS
— on pollination.
* Hose down tomatoes.
* Use a hairdryer (on cold) to help strawberry pollination.

1 metre length down into the frame so it overlaps the inside of the funnel. The piece sticking out of the top is folded outwards over the top ring after making several vertical cuts in it with scissors. Finally, a few layers of non-corrosive mesh, such as shadecloth, should be pushed inside the funnel to act as a filter and prevent later escape of medium.

If black plastic sheeting is to be used you will need a piece 1 metre square (40 inches square) and additional support will have to be added to the sides of the frame. A simple and attractive way to do this is to use a piece of plastic trellis 70 by 70 cm (27 1/2 by 27 1/2 in) with 5 by 5 cm (2 by 2 in) holes. Small trellis holes may make it too difficult to insert the strawberry plants. The trellis is wrapped around the frame and can easily be attached with plastic-coated wire. If you don't have plastic trellis you can use wire trellis or even chicken wire because the wire will be on the outside of the bag and the metal will not come into contact with the nutrient solution.

Once the trellis has been attached to the frame

medium to the next level at which a plant is to be inserted. In this fashion, fill the whole bag with medium interspersed with the roots of the plants.

Next, gently run water through the bag to remove any fine particles and to saturate the system. It must be stressed that the increase in weight of the whole bag may be surprising and it is best to place it in its permanent position before watering.

Ideally the bag should be suspended via a spindle so that it can be rotated for uniform exposure to sunlight. If you have difficulty buying a spindle you can use the kind of rotating clip which is fastened to the ends of dog leads or tethers. These can be bought from hardware stores. I have, on occasions, used a small electric motor to cause regular rotation, but this seems unnecessary if the light is adequate.

When the planted strawberry bag has been thoroughly washed and drained out, it may be connected to the circulating hydroponic system. Alternatively, the nutrient solution can be collected in a bucket underneath and poured back into the bag once or twice a day. Once the plants have been correctly planted and regularly fed (and hopefully rotated), then the system needs very little attention other than picking the strawberries and removing dead leaves and runners. Like just about any other type of hydroponic plant, the growth of strawberries in the cooler months of the year will be far more satisfactory if the bag is set up under optimal glasshouse conditions.

Panda film, which is black on the inside to prevent the sunlight stimulating algae growth inside the bag and white on the outside to reduce excessive heating of the root system, is now available. Black/white sheeting suitable for use in these strawberry bags instead of black sheeting can also be obtained from Hydroponic City (see Appendix). However, if the plants are looked after properly, by early summer most of the bag will be a mass of greenery which will prevent the plants overheating.

It is worth purchasing the best quality viral-free strawberry runners and these can usually be ordered from nurseries early in winter. Every trace of the old plants should be removed before the new stock is planted to prevent the spread of disease. Traditionally, strawberries produce their best crop in their second (and last) year. However,

in good hydroponic conditions, the yield obtained in the first year hardly bears criticism.

If I were to take the plunge and venture into commercial hydroponic strawberry growing, I would be reasonably confident of success with my vertical bags and I would not consider any other system in the light of experience to date. One bag provides two dozen plants producing abundant fruit in a very compact area which allows for very comfortable harvesting. Every house should have one.

Flowers

Flowers take to hydroponics like ducks to water! Any common flower does very well and some of the more adventurous hydroponicers are trying rarer species. The potential for producing beautiful displays of hydroponic plants appears unlimited. The following are a few examples of hydroponic successes.

Carnations (highly recommended)

Many of the long-stemmed Sim carnations sold by Australian florists are raised hydroponically. Such a beautiful end product may be beyond the amateur, but with care a supply of very fair specimens can be grown. One can start with seeds but generally cuttings or plants are preferable. These can be obtained from florist's shops or disease-free plants can be bought from specialist suppliers (see Appendix). Cuttings are usually grown in trays 25 by 36 cm (10 by 14 in) and 10 cm (4 in) deep. Three cuttings are planted per tray.

Before transplanting the cuttings into the system a suitable support can be made of two or three horizontal layers of fine, very open wire mesh, say, 15 cm (6 in) above each other. The plants can then be directed up through the mesh and the flowers easily cut. These layers of mesh should be installed before planting as the plants can easily be accidentally damaged by most constructors.

Carnations do well in most mediums provided feeding is regular and drainage excellent. Scoria, perlite or growool slabs are all successful. Left to their own devices, carnations will spread in a spindly fashion in all directions. This must not be allowed to happen as it will result in diseased bushes and small flowers. Therefore, when the plant has a height of about 15 cm (6 in), its top should be cut to encourage lateral growth. These potentially flower-bearing shoots can be subsequently guided upwards through the wire mesh. Any straggling growth, not inclined to shoot up vertically, should be removed.

Commercial carnation growers are dependent upon rigid disease prevention rather than disease control. The amateur should bear this in mind, as highly successful growing of carnations requires isolation procedures and the regular use of appropriate chemical sprays which is far from attractive to some people.

See also Epilogue.

Roses

In recent years the cut rose industry, particularly in Victoria, has swung dramatically to hydroponics. Roses seem to produce more prolifically and for a longer period in a hydroponic system. I cannot fault the results obtained to date using either perlite or granulated growool in plastic buckets or drums. My only

Above right: Sim carnations produce continuously for months on end. Individual stems need careful cutting back to base as the flower matures.

Right: Hydroponic roses growing in plastic drums filled with perlite.

Far right: Sweet peas.

A DINING ROOM TABLE SETTING

<u>A</u> A hydroponic petunia
grown in vermiculite and
ready for the vase.

<u>B</u> Preparing for the table.

<u>C</u> Being admired by a guest.

advice is to give roses plenty of room because the water shoot and flower production can be phenomenal.

Sweet Peas (highly recommended)

Dwarf sweet peas are bliss to grow and the only attention they need is about 30 cm (12 in) of support. They grow equally well in either perlite or growool. The seedlings can be raised in a germination incubator or the seed sown onto the medium and lightly covered with paper until it has germinated.

The usual climbing varieties, if planted in a couple of metres (several yards) of plastic guttering and given daily manual feeding, make a splendid hydroponic display. The nutrient solution can be drained back into a bucket and hence a simple recycling system established. Such a system is ideal for sweet peas since it can be set up in any sheltered sunny position. For an even prettier effect, a row of dwarf sweet peas can be planted in front of the climbers, so that there is a solid mass of flowers.

Flowers in Hydrotubes

Beautiful displays can be achieved in tubes filled with growool. A particularly attractive one is a mixture of miniature dahlias and lobelia. There are many combinations which can be explored. Seeds and bulbs can also be planted in hydrotubes (Chapter 4).

Orchids and Carnivorous Plants

The special food and pH requirements of orchids can be achieved hydroponically but they naturally cannot be incorporated into a standard recirculating hydroponic system. Carnivorous plants generally require no circulating nutrients, only the purest quality water available. They come in very handy for pest and disease control (see Chapter 8).

CHAPTER 7

Maintenance of Hydroponic Systems and Care of the Plant's Environment

Observation — Look, Listen, Sniff and Touch

Look

Hydroponic plants are entirely dependent upon humans and they have many ways of signalling their distress. Like a surgeon, the hydroponicer must have the eyes of an eagle as he or she regularly and intelligently inspects both plants and equipment. Drooping new growth may indicate water shortage and/or excessive heat. Early signs of mineral deficiency should be sought out (see

Chapter 2). Pests usually strike on the underside of leaves first and these should be regularly inspected. Plants that are diseased or infected should be promptly dealt with and aged or dead plants and foliage removed.

Every time you clap eyes on your hydroponic garden, scan it very closely. A little or big plant may be trying to tell you something. By its very nature, things move very quickly in hydroponics. As my father always used to inspect the chooks when he got home from work, I tend always to have a short prowl around the hydroponic system.

Listen

The sounds of hydroponics may give a timely warning. A change in the tone of an electric pump may forewarn of bearing or impeller damage and should be promptly replaced. The deathly hush of a burnt-out motor on a hot day is an enthusiast's nightmare. A new sound of dripping may disclose a loosened fitting or overflow due to a blocked outlet. Such leaks seem to occur in remote and partially inaccessible corners and may go for weeks without detection unless one is alert.

Sniff

To my surprise, in 1984 when William Bliss inspected my set-up, his final act was to dive his hands deep into the medium and have a good sniff of the samples. A healthy well-drained medium, he said, should smell fresh. With a bit of sniffing about one can soon

A PLANT GROWING HYDROPONICALLY IS ENTIRELY DEPENDENT ON HUMAN CARE.

A poor basil drooping due to lack of water (the supply dripper had blocked).

A midsummer tragedy. Death of tomato plants after a pump failure which went unnoticed for four days.

> **HYDROHINT**
> All hydroponic systems should be flushed through regularly. This includes both the tubing and the mediums. Flushing the tubing through will remove precipitated and other matter which can lead to dripper blockage. Flushing clean water through the medium will reduce the build up of salts which can be damaging to plants.

detect any areas of poor drainage, which may encourage harmful bacterial growth as well as harm plants in the vicinity.

Touch

After the nutrient has drained away, the medium should be moist but not dripping wet. If perlite crumbles upon rubbing, then it is too dry.

Supply of Nutrient Solution

1 Non-recycling Systems

Usually nutrient solution should be applied once daily during the slow growth period and twice in warmer weather. The quantity will depend entirely upon the size and type of the container and the plant therein. For example, a mature tomato plant growing in a laundry bucket should be fed 1 litre (0.26 US gal) of solution twice a day in very hot weather.

The nutrient solution also plays a role in flushing out excess salts from the medium. From time to time extra nutrient solution, or water alone, should be applied so that this flushing action occurs.

In extremely hot weather you may have to water the containers as well as protect them from direct sunlight. Signs of wilting indicate the need for more watering and, provided drainage is adequate, excess watering to be on the safe side can do no harm in the short term. The nutrient can be replaced later in the day. In other words, the urgent demand is for plenty of water and the brief shortage of nutrients does little harm.

2 Recycling Systems

For maintenance of manual recycling systems see Chapter 4, pages 38–41.

Recycling nutrients — how often?

Some systems, especially small ones, run continuously and provided drainage is very good this can do no harm. In particular the nutrient film technique (Chapter 4) often uses a continuous twenty-four hour flow.

I prefer pulse feeding and in summer the timer starts the pump at regular intervals between the hours of 7.30 a.m. and 7 p.m. The timer is usually set to activate the pump for five minutes at fifteen minute intervals. This allows good wetting of the medium and adequate time for drainage. The lateness of the final feeding allows me to check that all is well when I get home from work.

Recycling nutrients — how much?

Sufficient nutrient should flow through the medium to keep it moist at all times. As with non-recycling systems, if drainage is good then one cannot oversupply the nutrient solution. Naturally, the larger the container the greater the required flow from a dripper. Very large containers, for example garbage bins, will require supply from several drippers.

Replacement of water used

Most people don't have to remember to add fresh water regularly since it is so easy to fit a ballcock and reservoir or direct hose link (page 44) to the drainage tank. However, if hand filling of the tank is required then a routine must be adhered to, particularly in hot weather when a large quantity of water is taken up by the plants as well as being lost by evaporation from the surface of the medium. When hand filling your tank turn the recirculating system off and allow all the water to drain back first. However, if your system keeps the pump going continuously, you can fill the tank while it is running.

Nutrients

In any recycling system the nutrient solution should be replaced at least every four weeks. Some authorities recommend replacement every two weeks in summer and monthly in winter. In the author's system (page 16), nutrient solution is made up at one-half strength and to maintain this level during periods of rapid growth extra nutrient has to be added every second or third day. At other times, once a week may be adequate. After twenty-eight days all the nutrient solution is pumped onto the garden and replaced.

In periods of active growth the electroconductivity of the nutrient solution (see page 12) should be checked every second day and adjustments

> **HYDROHINT**
> Very important. Promptly remove sick or aging plants from the system.

made as appropriate. The pH (see page 13) of the nutrient solution should be checked weekly and, if it has risen too high, the nutrient solution be replaced rather than adjusted with the addition of acid.

Cleansing the system with fresh water

Every two months copious amounts of fresh water should be circulated through the system to remove mineral build-up. As well, the surface medium should be hosed thoroughly and then all returned water discarded.

At this time all drippers should be disassembled and scrubbed out. An old toothbrush and dilute soapy water helps to remove encrusted material.

Sterilisation of the medium

There is really no point in the amateur hydroponicer attempting this procedure. It is a different matter for commercial producers who desire to eradicate completely certain pathogens and pests from their plants using appropriately designed steam sterilisers, etc. The amateur is unlikely to carry out successful sterilisation and sterility, like pregnancy, is an absolute state so 'almost' sterilising the medium defeats the purpose. The other argument against the amateur attempting sterilisation of mediums is that contamination will inevitably recur, possibly within days.

Filters

Filters incorporated in the tubing distributing the nutrient solution should be cleaned monthly. In addition I direct the returning nutrient through a plastic kitchen sieve layered with aquarium filter polyester. This lining is changed weekly as it most efficiently collects a great deal of debris. Since I adopted this system blockage of tubing and drippers has been reduced.

Temperature of the nutrient solution

The ideal temperature range is from 18 to 24°C (64 to 75°F). In cold climates, a submersible heater may be used to warm the solution.

Avoiding a Dry Atmosphere

Provided ventilation is adequate, all plants mentioned in this book like a bit of moisture in the atmosphere. They will not thrive in a bone-dry environment. Therefore, the humidity in a glasshouse or plastic house should be raised regularly by hosing down the plants and their surroundings. This also makes them look good, brings down dead foliage which can later be swept up and helps with the pollination of some plants, especially tomatoes. Cheap automatic misting equipment is available (see Epilogue).

Plant Grooming and Training

One of the pleasures of hydroponics lies in the skilful tidying up of plants. Dead or ageing leaves should be removed and excess or misdirected growth pruned. Such grooming allows better air movement around the plants and reduces susceptibility to diseases such as mildew. Plants such as tomatoes benefit from a precise pruning and training programme which is relatively simple (see page 68).

A good supply of flexible ties should always be on hand to train and support the plants.

Harvesting of Crops

A mental note should be taken of the plants which are nearly ready to yield their fruit. As a general rule, the sooner ripe or near ripe produce is removed, the greater the overall yield from the plant. It is an unfortunate fact that when hydroponic systems are inspected there is often in evidence much overripe or gone-to-seed material.

It is sensible to have a container always on hand for the harvest and to keep the household informed on progress. Ideally, meals can be planned around the seasonal produce of the hydroponic garden. Try to grow plants or herbs which will delight your family.

Removal of Old or Dying Plants

Sadly, one must be ruthless and the moment the useful life of a plant has passed, it and as much of its root system as possible must be removed. Failure to do so wastes space and growing time. Moreover, these plants are prone to disease and pests, and may reduce the quality of the nutrient solution. Often plants are left in the system for far too long and this fault may be corrected by having a predetermined but slightly flexible planting programme.

Replacement of Plants

In the warmer months many plants can be immediately replaced either with seeds or seedlings. This is especially the case with lettuces and dwarf French beans.

Crop rotation is not necessary in hydroponics and one can replace the same type of plant at the site of its predecessor.

Root Penetration

Even if well fed, some plants take particular delight in sending roots out through drainage pipes which may then become obstructed. Horseradish and mint are often the offenders and their attempts should be regularly thwarted. Of course, plants that are being starved will send

HARVESTING CROPS

<u>A</u> Mature cylindrical beetroot.

<u>B</u> These potatoes were grown in growool.

<u>C</u> Leeks are an excellent standby for a cook because they grow steadily over a long period and can be harvested as required.

<u>D</u> Parsnips can be plucked out of the medium (usually perlite) as required; they have a delightful bouquet and are not woody like many earth-grown parsnips.

<u>E</u> Hydroponic squash, ready for dinner.

exploratory roots off in any promising direction. Any excessive root penetration, therefore, suggests inadequate feeding.

Pest and Disease Control

Most commercial hydroponicers have a spraying or fumigation routine. Although healthy fast-growing plants are less susceptible to pests and disease, it is clear that to succeed with certain plants some preventive measures must be taken. A spraying programme is essential even in a glasshouse or igloo protected by large insect-proof wire doors and vents, and certain plants, like broccoli, if grown in an unprotected outside system, will be eaten within days by pests unless sprayed regularly. The sprays which you use will depend upon whether you prefer natural insecticides or potent modern chemicals.

Whatever agents are used, they should be applied at least monthly. Some authorities recommend fortnightly applications. The writer originally adopted a programme of spraying monthly all appropriate plants with a complete garden spray

and fumigating the igloo with dichlorvos at the same interval (see Chapter 8).

In recent years, I have tried to reduce the use of potent insecticides by accepting insect pests as a part of life, and have taken measures to control their numbers rather than eliminate them completely (see Chapter 8).

Protection from Excessive Heat

Many plants will only briefly tolerate temperatures over 35°C (95°F), and then only if they have adequate water and their roots are kept cool. In very hot weather an outside hydroponic system performs much better if protected by some type of shadecloth. Even a temporary measure, like covering plants with an old sheet, may save the more delicate ones. If plants are grown in black containers and exposed to very hot sun, it is almost certain that the outer roots will be baked. The only sure protection on a fierce summer's day is good shadecloth and plenty of hosing down, combined with adequate air circulation.

Glasshouses and igloos easily overheat in summer unless precautions are taken. Most commercial establishments paint the roofs and walls

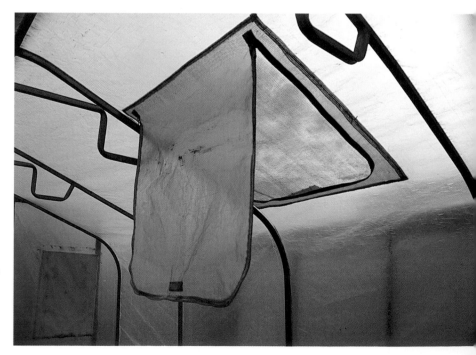

A good idea for ventilation: this small commercial igloo photographed at One Stop Sprinklers has a zippered ceiling vent which is also fitted with a fly-screen.

white and install electrically powered ventilation triggered by thermostats. The very sophisticated ones may have air-conditioning. The amateur must also realise that, to prevent a glasshouse becoming a positive oven in summer, preparations must be made to cope with both moderate and heatwave conditions. There are several ways of reducing the temperature.

Firstly, there should be adequate vents to allow good airflow through the unit, as well as extra vents to be opened when the sun becomes excessively hot. It may be necessary to use a large fan to aid circulation of air and this should be well protected if you use a misting system. In smaller units an exhaust fan is usually unnecessary as adequate vents will do the job. The details of a venting system for an igloo are given on page 122.

Secondly, some reflective painting and/or shadecloth is essential. Greenhouse white paint which is slowly removed by rain and wind tends to be unpleasing to the eye in a back garden. It is better to use a more permanent white or off-white paint on part of the glasshouse or igloo and make a cover of some sort to slide over a portion of the unpainted surface when hot weather is approaching. Covers can be made of calico, canvas or shadecloth. The painting of igloos and use of covers is considered on page 121.

Thirdly, the use of an automatic misting system is a great help in lowering the temperature, provided ventilation is adequate. On a very hot day the regular misting of the interior of an igloo may, by evaporation, keep the temperature significantly below that outside. Apart from evaporative cooling, the misting reduces the chances of plant dehydration. Misting systems are discussed on pages 113–4 and 122.

Finally, if water-filled 'heat banks' are employed they will absorb a lot of heat during the day and release it at night. There is more about heat banks below.

Heating the Plant's Environment

It is the dream of many a gardener to have a heated glasshouse or polyhouse so that rapid growth of plants can be maintained all year.

Manufacturers do cater for the enthusiast who wants automatic gas or electric heating of a small glasshouse or polyhouse. However, equipment and running costs can be very high and well beyond the means of most amateurs. Putting in insulated inner walls or special covers will reduce heat loss and hence power bills. There are also more and more experimental heating units run on solar power and others which make use of methane tapped from garbage deposits.

HYDROHINT
Establish a maintenance/routine that you are comfortable with. More attention will be required during times of rapid growth which is a most exciting time anyway!

For most of us who have to make do without artificial heating there is one simple way to provide some natural heating and that is by using water-filled 'heat banks'. It is estimated that at least 90 per cent of the radiant heat from the sun entering a glasshouse or igloo is rapidly lost. If black water-filled drums are placed inside a glasshouse they will absorb the radiant heat. Later, when the day cools, this stored energy will be released and heat the air around the drums. Apart from being a splendid environmentally friendly way to store and release heat, the water banks help to cool the glasshouse on hot days. You should install as many of these black painted drums as you have room for.

Once you start looking for empty black plastic drums, you or your acquaintances will soon find them. Many factories, hospitals, etc., have available lots of suitable non-returnable containers that are there for the asking. Care should be taken that they don't contain traces of dangerous chemicals.

Many commercial growers use water-filled black plastic sausages running in rows along the floors of their units, and you can obtain this plastic tubing from most large horticultural suppliers (see pages 129–36). The heavier duty material is the better buy as it is less easily punctured. This tougher tubing can also be used for the vertical culture of strawberries (see page 74).

This use of black drums or tubing is highly recommended since both tend to even out temperature fluctuations. On a cool summer evening the release of heat can be quite striking.

Use of Artificial Lights

There have been great advances in both the type and efficiency of artificial lights in recent years. The availability of high-intensity discharge lamps, especially high pressure sodium lamps, has had enormous impact on greenhouse horticulture, and especially hydroponics. Amateur hydroponicers, especially those living in cooler climes, should investigate these lights. Most retail hydroponic outlets sell, or can obtain, appropriate lighting kits for the customer. Superficially, the variety of high density discharge lamps available may seem daunting. For example, one large firm, Greenlite, lists some thirty-three types of lamps, although these are designed to cater for a wide range of specialist crops and conditions. However, with good advice the amateur can set up a nice little artificial sun to encourage plant growth in winter inside his or her glasshouse or spare room. A popular artificial lighting system is described below.

The lighting requirements of plants is a fascinating science which has brought enormous benefits. On one hand, the yield of flowers and, most important, the time of their maturation can be controlled, and on the other hand many vegetables and other crops can be grown successfully indoors all the year round. From such extremes as Antarctic bases to small blacked out rooms in Kings Cross, Sydney, crops grow vigorously under artificial lights. In Europe and elsewhere, many thousands of hectares of greenhouses maintain non-stop crop production by making up for the weakness of the winter sun. Brisk and predictable plant production can be maintained, thanks to the ability to fine-tune the artificial lighting used to suit the particular plant or plants involved.

The two parts of visible light from sunshine most needed by the plants are the orange–red component and, at the other end of the light

HYDROHINTS

Special care of artificial lights—
* Never touch the hot bulb.
* Keep water, sprays, etc., away from the lamp fitting at all times.

<u>A</u> The author's artificial light encourages vigorous plant growth in winter.

<u>B</u> An attractive extended sunset in the garden thanks to artificial light.

spectrum, the blue light component. Blue light positively attracts a plant. The plant will lean and grow towards the light, spreading its leaves to enhance the light's absorption. The orange–red component is vital for photosynthesis and hence growth.

Plant physiologists have worked out the best conditions for the various stages of growth of most commercial crops. The two main variables they have concentrated on in the use of artificial supplemental lighting is the composition of the light itself, and the duration to which the plants are exposed to it.

The following generalisations hold true for most plants:

> Seedlings and young plants will benefit from a longer exposure to light. On the other hand, flower production may be slowed down by a short nocturnal burst of light, thus allowing the producer to time the crop, say chrysanthemums, to precisely target Mother's Day. If using artificial lighting to promote plant growth it will give better results if used after the sun has set. Most plants, such as vegetable and summer-blooming plants, will thrive on this extra energy source provided they have four to six hours of darkness in each twenty-four hour cycle. Longer periods of lighting will not result in additional growth.

Selection of Artificial Lighting Equipment

High pressure sodium lamps are the obvious choice for the home hydroponicer and they really can turn night into day.

The unit I have bought uses a Phillips SON-T AGRO of 400 watts. This type of lamp is one of the most popular ones in Australia at the moment. Its manufacturers claim it is an improvement on earlier sodium lamps and all crops, ranging from tomatoes to chrysanthemums, respond better to its use. Lamps of 1000 watts are also available.

The unit cost A$300 and was a good invest-

ment. It consisted of a heavy ballast, the lamp and lamp housing and an adjustable reflector.

The ballast provides the initial burst of high voltage to vaporise the sodium and mercury which is in the inner tube of the sodium lamp. It then goes on to supply an even level of power. It takes some five minutes for the light to warm up to 90 per cent brightness. A hot light needs to cool down somewhat before it will restart.

Installation of the equipment is simple but, as with all other electricals, it must be safe, well earthed, away from moisture and preferably with a safety switch. It is sensible to install a timing device at the same time.

Care of the lamp itself deserves special note. Make sure it is screwed in properly and, whilst cold, wipe off any finger prints. It is a good idea to wipe it down every two weeks or so as any dirt will reduce its efficiency. The light is extraordinarily bright and should not be looked at directly.

Care should be taken not to bump the lamp when it has been used for some time because its internal parts become more brittle. A jolt may reduce its life expectancy to less than the average 16 000 hours.

The light should not be placed closer to plants than 30 cm (12 in) whilst seedlings should be kept from 60 to 90 cm (2 to 3 ft) distant. Ideally the plants may be moved around regularly to allow even distribution of light and, hence, more even growth.

> **HYDROHINT**
> Feed important and/or large plants via two drippers to offset the danger of dripper blockage.

Maintenance of Records

A record of dates of sowing seeds, planting out, harvesting and then removal of plants will prove invaluable in determining next season's plans. Details of nutrient solution changes or additions, dates and types of spray or fumigation should all be recorded. The process only takes a few seconds if a ballpoint pen attached to a notebook is kept handy. A China pencil is ideal for marking dates, etc., on plastic and other containers.

Annual Clean-up

In many parts of the world hydroponics comes to a near halt in winter, unless some type of heating and/or artificial lighting is used. This is an excellent time to close down for a thorough clean-up. When all the plants and their roots and debris have been removed the whole system can be sterilised by circulating a diluted solution of sodium hypochlorite overnight, making sure that the medium is well saturated. Household bleach

---

HYDROHINTS

Keep pests out. Close insect-proof doors promptly, etc. Take care outside insects are not introduced via garden tools, etc. A clean and tidy hydroponic garden will usually yield bountiful rewards.

---

such as White King diluted 1:40 in water is quite suitable provided care is taken to avoid contact with eyes or skin. The precautions printed on the label of this corrosive substance should be closely followed.

Next day extensive flushing with fresh water is necessary because residual bleach will be toxic to plants.

For gardeners with small hydroponic kits, it is best to throw out all the old medium, nutrients, etc., and just clean the equipment in a bath of diluted household bleach. Remember to rinse it afterwards. Then restart the kit with new materials.

Some people use appropriately diluted swimming pool chlorine preparations for medium sterilisation and again a thorough flushing out is required afterwards. Formalin is used in some commercial hydroponic establishments but this is not recommended for the

---

HYDROHINT

Don't overcrowd your plants. This will lead to disappointing results.

---

amateur. Steam sterilisation is employed by some growers.

Finally, there is no point in sterilising a hydroponic system and then reconnecting an established plant in its container filled with 'old' untreated medium. Any contamination in the old medium will promptly spread throughout the system. Thus you must either discard all the plants and sterilise all the medium at the one time or decide not to undertake any sterilisation. I now believe sterilisation should be left to the larger commercial outfits and is not necessary for hobby hydroponicers.

Disadvantages of Glasshouses and Igloos

Never forget that once a plant is taken indoors rain will not reach it, nor will it usually be accessible to insect predators such as birds, spiders and the odd praying mantis.

To the human, the confined space of a poorly ventilated igloo or glasshouse may be dangerous. Careless use of sprays may result in absorption of toxins and even be fatal. Serious illness can sometimes result from the excessive inhalation of dried fungal spores. Other respiratory problems such as asthma may be precipitated because of the build up of dried plant products. Last, but not least, is the danger posed by electrical circuits which are not waterproofed and fitted with cut-out safety mechanisms.

I know of one man who suffered a life-threatening fungal infection as a result of cleaning up a poorly ventilated glasshouse. The infection was due to *Aspergillus* and he was left with permanent lung damage. Plenty of ventilation and hosing everything down before cleaning up should eliminate such risks. If in doubt, always use an appropriate mask.

CHAPTER 8

Pest and Disease Control

Healthy, rapidly growing hydroponic plants are usually less prone to many infestations and diseases than conventionally grown plants. Nevertheless, various invaders, if given the opportunity, may insidiously or dramatically attack one's current pride and joy. Fortunately, a positive approach to the problem may reduce heartbreak and disappointment.

The use of pesticides is a hot issue which is far from resolved. Many commercial producers, perhaps egged on by their bank managers, adhere to regular programmes using highly potent chemical sprays. As natural resistance to these chemicals develop, markets open for new and more potent insecticides. On the other end of the scale, there are those who use only natural or environmentally friendly methods of pest control which may prove of limited value.

Whereas some years back I aimed for total elimination of pests, I am now comfortable with a compromise situation.

The measures outlined below reduce the likelihood of bugs having what they think is their fair share of the crop. They advise the use of quite acceptable and simple sprays to make the insects' lives unpleasant and reduce or even eliminate them.

Isolation of Clean Plants

As mentioned in Chapter 7, pest control for plants grown out in the open is far more difficult than for those raised in an environment protected by wire screening. Diseases spread by insects are also reduced by such barriers. However, even when very strict measures, as carried out by some commercial carnation growers, are taken to isolate disease-free healthy plants, routine spraying is still necessary because of the difficulty of excluding small disease-carrying insects like mites and thrips.

Once the growing area has been protected by wire screening then the adoption of some simple rules will dramatically enhance the health of most plants. As far as possible raise all plants from good quality seeds inside the unit. Seeds marketed by reputable firms are usually free from any problems and ensure that healthy plants spring to life. Avoid introducing any plants from outside unless you are sure they are healthy and free from pests and disease. As soon as plants are past their prime they should be removed. Very often an elderly or dying plant will become a focus for some disease or parasite which may spread to neighbouring plants. As stressed in Chapter 7, it is essential to remove old or fallen foliage regularly and intelligently prune and train plants.

Thus, a clean and tidy unit can be established with the one-way progression of plants from seeds to maturity to prompt disposal. Even without the use of pesticides, the results obtained will be dramatically better than when the plants are unprotected from their many natural enemies.

> **HYDROHINT**
> I dip my secateurs in a jar of methylated spirits before and after use. Some experts recommend the use of household bleach for disinfecting glasshouse tools. This is prepared by adding 150 ml (5.2 oz) of 4 per cent sodium hypochlorite to 1 litre (0.26 US gal) of water.
> Note: Keep these disinfectant solutions away from children.

Hot House and Igloo Tools, etc.

There is no point in going to considerable pains to isolate your hydroponic plants and then employing secateurs or other tools which have just been used on your outside plants. This is a sure way to spread disease, especially with secateurs which will transfer material from one cut surface to another. Cleanliness and convenience are both served by having a set of small tools which is only used inside the unit. Secateurs, scissors and pliers along with ties and other bits and pieces should be kept in a central waterproof container.

Plant Diseases and Pests

Plants grown hydroponically can suffer from all the diseases and parasites of conventionally raised plants. Only a brief outline of the subject is given here and the reader should consult a good gardening book for a detailed account (see the Bibliography). Excellent garden advisory centres are located in most states and their staff will give helpful and authoritative guidance to all gardeners. If a sample of the plant causing concern is taken to one of these centres, a precise diagnosis as well as recommended treatment is usually forthcoming. Many a problem can be sorted out by talking to someone at one's local nursery but sometimes, especially when an important crop is involved, the full-time expert should be hurriedly consulted.

There are many viruses and fungi which attack plants. The common fungi are rust, mildew and moulds.

Plant Viruses

Most plant viruses are spread from one plant to another by sucking insects such as aphids. Once a plant is infected with a virus there is no treatment and it should be removed immediately. Seeds are usually considered to be virus free and many nurseries stock virus-free plants. If these are introduced into a clean area with good insect eradication then virus disease may be avoided. Strawberry plants are usually sold as virus-free stock. Viruses reproduce within the living cells of the plant and, although the plant does not necessarily die, it may be ruined by viral spread.

Fungal Diseases

There are many of these diseases and every plant seems to be a special target at some time in its life. Fungae are primitive microscopic plants which parasitise larger plants in huge numbers. The names of the diseases they cause are highly descriptive of the havoc they can produce. Consider the following: black spot, canker, collar rot, downy mildew, leaf curl and rust. The ominous ring of some of these foretells crop failure. However, with well ventilated, healthy plants and judicial use of fungicidal sprays many fungal diseases can be controlled. The selection of fungal-resistant strains and prompt removal of old or diseased plants reduce the risk further. Overcrowding of plants is an invitation for fungal invasion.

The use of fungicides is considered under spraying programmes below.

Plant Pests

Snails and slugs are very fond of nice juicy hydroponic plants, especially those growing near ground level. In such situations the scattering of a few pellets of a modern snail bait such as Baysol is advisable. Bait should be used sparsely and never in heaps, as this is wasteful and may lead to the poisoning of pets or birds. A layer of coarse sand can be a good barrier to the movement of snails. If you keep the area free of potential snail homes, such as empty plant containers, you will increase the trek these pests must make to feed. An occasional summer night patrol with a torch is recommended.

Leaf-eating and sap-sucking insects
Each kind of plant has at least one major insect enemy and the healthiest plant can be overwhelmed by the sheer numbers of insects feeding upon it. Most gardeners easily recognise the more obvious pests like aphids, cabbage butterflies and moths. The

> **HYDROHINT**
> Fungal diseases will rarely attack healthy, well-ventilated, uncrowded plants.

SPOT THE CULPRIT

<u>A</u> Very healthy basil being eaten.

<u>B</u> The basil-filled culprit immediately before execution.

Grub sneakily at work on the underside of a silverbeet leaf.

more minute creatures like the two-spotted mite (red spider mite), which can be equally devastating, are less obvious. Details of common pests are found in most good gardening books (see the Bibliography) and, as with plant diseases, professional advice is usually quite easy to find.

Pests like cutworms and wireworms that spend part of their life cycle in soil are avoided in hydroponics. Furthermore, many species can be almost totally excluded by insect screening around the hydroponic unit. However, very few gardeners have consistent success without the use of some sort of insecticide.

Spotting the Culprit(s)

A lot of pests are masters of disguise. The colour of grubs may range from a luscious leaf green to that of a dried brown stem. Viewed from a metre (or yard) away, they tend to be invisible. White flies can lurk in their hundreds on the underside of foliage as may millions of the tiny two-spotted mite.

Companion Planting

Some plants repel insects to various degrees. For example, basil planted near tomatoes is said to reduce the incidence of whitefly. My experience has been that whitefly are quite partial to basil, but I still persist with this ritual because people I respect say it works.

Companion planting is effective to a varying degree and discourages insect pests rather than eliminating them. The subject is quite complicated and the mechanisms vary. For example, the scent of a plant may be off-putting to the insect or it

THE ENEMY MAY BE SPOTTED BY ADOPTING THE FOLLOWING ROUTINE.

* Inspect plants closely once a week. If something's obviously been eating the foliage, it's probably still there and you can try to spot it. Often grubs will tackle the newest growth in preference to the old.

* The droppings from grubs can be a dead give-away. White plastic spread below a tomato plant can accurately pinpoint the position of a voracious tomato grub. It's very satisfactory to pick it off and, after disposing of it, hose the plastic down. The appearance of additional droppings is usually the stimulus to reach for the pyrethrum spray.

* Shaking the foliage of plants may render the enemy airborne and more visible. This is especially the case with whitefly which concentrate on new growth.

* If a plant is sickly, inspection with a magnifying glass may reveal the cause. With magnification, it is easy to spot the all-too-common two-spotted mite. This tiny little eight-legged creature does enormous damage to azaleas, roses, tomatoes and many other plants. When foliage has been misted, the mite's delicate, but dense, webbing may be seen.

A Telltale droppings spotted on white plastic lying under tomato plants.

B The source of the droppings seen in the dead centre of the picture. A pyrethrum spray was used promptly.

may attract the insect's predators. Another plant may fix nitrogen which is an advantage to nearby plants. Companion planting has limited application in hydroponics but may be of considerable benefit to the conventional gardener. Jackie French has written an excellent book on this subject (see Bibliography).

To Spray or not To Spray?

For years people have attempted to protect their crops from insects, but it is only with the advent of potent modern pesticides in spite of their disadvantages that control can usually be ensured until harvest. Nowadays, however, many consumers are strongly opposed to the use of chemical sprays because of their environmental effects and possible contamination of the end product.

The excessive use of a powerful pesticide may even worsen the situation by wiping out a pest's natural predators. Pests may develop resistance to insecticides but they never develop resistance to a spider's fangs or a quick peck from a bird's beak. It was once estimated that the weight of insects destroyed by the spider population of England and Wales each year exceeded the total weight of the human populations in those two regions!

This is as true for the home enthusiast as the market gardener and no gardener should kill these pollution-free automatic insect destroyers — unless they are funnel-web spiders or red-back spiders! However, spiders don't do too well in a glasshouse and on a hot day I find the odd huntsman has swooned from the heat. As described below, carnivorous plants can discreetly reduce insect numbers.

Suggested Programme of Insect Control

When all the conditions necessary to keep the plants healthy have been established and surveillance of them has become automatic, the following routine can be followed.

1 At least once a week, give all plants a regular hose-down, especially on the undersurface of the foliage. In hot weather this should be done more frequently and, provided ventilation is adequate, the plants will love it. Lately I have tended also to spray the foliage more frequently with a mist of nutrient solution (see page 46) to encourage growth.

   My hydroponic roses improved no end merely by this regular wetting. If they go for weeks without such treatment, they are overwhelmed by the dryness-loving spotted spider mite.

2 Organic soap sprays are my first line of attack and are only used when some pest is in evidence.

   There are a number of safe preparations available. Examples are *Clensil, Natrasoap* and *Safer*. The spray has to make direct contact with the soft-bodied insect to be effective. It may not destroy eggs and so, when hatching has

occurred, further spraying will be necessary. Clensil contains citronella oil and it leaves my hydroponic plants with a lovely clean smell which is in marked contrast to some other sprays which frankly stink!

Soap sprays may not wipe out all insects pests but they certainly make life near intolerable for the main offenders. The populations of aphids, two-spotted mites, thrips, whiteflies and juicy grubs will be decimated by the regular use of soap sprays.

3 Pyrethrins are extracted from the flowers of a particular chrysanthemum and are acceptable pesticides for organic gardeners. Their cultivation is a big and attractive industry in Tasmania. Safe synthetic pyrethrins are also available.

   This is a contact spray which works rapidly on a wide variety of insects. It is of very low toxicity to people and animals. Sunlight destroys its activity after a few hours and the withholding period after spraying crops is only one day.

   I use pyrethrin when things are getting a little out of hand. For example, if a concentration of whiteflies are found to be having a picnic on a young extension of a tomato plant they will be hit by pyrethrin. A little hand pump dispenser is on standby for this purpose. If pyrethrin is to be used on a regular basis, it's economic sense to buy the concentrate rather than the diluted preparation.

   Generally, it's better to spray the whole of the plant thoroughly with pyrethrin to reduce the net population and then attend to little pockets of resistance with a smaller hand-held spray.

4 As stated earlier, I have tended to move away from the stronger chemical sprays. An outbreak of leaf-feeding insects which threaten a crop may warrant the use of carbaryl. This is a

> **HYDROHINT**
> Check your plants from time to time late at night. Sometimes slugs and snails go to extreme lengths to reach luscious hydroponic plants for a midnight feast. Though uncommon, when it happens it's surprising how much damage one snail can do under the cover of darkness.

relatively safe contact insecticide and crops sprayed with it have a three day withholding period. I'm comfortable using carbaryl when it seems necessary and when I do use it I make sure that the plants are thoroughly and effectively sprayed.

Organophosphates such as Rogor (dimethoate) are absorbed, at least in part, by the plants and render its sap toxic to insects. They are also contact killers. I worry about the ready availability of such toxic compounds and use them rarely, highly selectively and following the manufacturers' instructions (see page 98).

Programmed Spraying

If chemical sprays are to be used on a regular basis, they should be carefully selected as an adjunct to providing the optimum conditions for healthy growth. As stressed earlier, the use of some type of screening to limit insect access is invaluable in pest reduction.

The amateur can use chemical sprays in either of two ways. He or she can wait until some infestation is clearly evident and then attack it. The

> **HYDROHINT**
> Use the gentlest of sprays whenever possible. Regardless of the type of spray always read and follow the instructions carefully. Resist the temptation add an 'extra dash'. This is wasteful and may harm the plants.

other and more successful approach is to introduce a seasonal spraying routine aimed at preventing pests or diseases getting a hold or at least keeping them under control.

To adopt, say, a fortnightly spraying routine may seem a lot of work but it will avoid the disruption caused by the discovery of some impending planticide on a Sunday morning. It takes a bit of research to determine a suitable spray combination and the right interval between spraying. One approach is to list all the plants you intend to grow and then hot foot it down to your local nursery for advice, preferably not during a busy period.

Many plants either don't need spraying or may be harmed by certain sprays. Once you have expert advice on what to spray and when, a quiet confidence in the eventual outcome is almost assured. Furthermore, you will not be guilty of indiscriminate use of chemical agents.

Fungicides

There are wide range of fungicides available, from the safe and faithful Bordeaux mixture to modern long-acting compounds that are not acceptable to organic gardeners. I get by with little loss and without their use, by having a rapid turnover of plants and selecting resistant strains when possible.

Environmentally Friendly Homemade Sprays

The best of these is pyrethrin which is not made from the common garden chrysanthemum but one which must be specially cultivated. There are many homemade pesticides in use — some are of doubtful effectiveness and/or more trouble than they are worth. In many of them any effect is probably attributable to the vegetable soap component. My dad used to make a powerful insecticide by soaking some old tobacco in soapy water. The highly toxic nicotine was quickly extracted from the tobacco and the brew would kill most bugs on first contact. Commercial nicotine sprays were withdrawn some years ago because they killed a few gardeners as well! It's important to realise that some homemade sprays, e.g. elder spray, can be quite toxic to humans.

Pesticide sprays can be made from a wide range of starting materials ranging from bugs, marigold and stinging nettles to the leaves of tomatoes, which are surprisingly toxic. A spray made from garlic may kill insects but they have to actually eat the preparation. This spray is also an effective fungicide, as apparently is seaweed extract. A range of recipes and their evaluation may be found in the book by Jackie French (see Bibliography).

Biological Control of Insects

There are now a number of companies specialising in biological control which distribute, for example, predatory mites which make quick work of two-spotted mites. For details of the predators and the companies, contact your local Department of Agriculture.

Carnivorous Plants

For years I've kept carnivorous plants. These little pets require little attention other than a regular drink of rainwater or distilled water. Tap water can kill them as it often contains salts which accumulate over time, etc. They grow successfully in one part vermiculite to four parts of peat moss and need no feeding.

Although the venus fly trap dispatches many an insect, the sundews seem particularly effective at fixing whiteflies.

Australian television's top gardening personality, Don Burke, is transfixed by some of the author's carnivorous plants. He impressed the author no end by recording an off-the-cuff segment on them.

PLANT TRAPS

<u>A</u> This large pitcher plant in a bucket has a fatal attraction for insects.

<u>B</u> Veined throat of the waiting pitcher plant.

PLANT TRAPS

A The hungry mouths of a venus fly trap.

B Crunch!

Manufacturers' Instructions and Safety Precautions

Pesticides and fungicides are poisons and can be highly dangerous to humans and animals. Instructions should be read carefully and followed precisely. A common error is to exceed the recommended concentration for good measure and this not only can damage the plants but is very wasteful. If any doubt exists about usage or compatibility of sprays, then ask the manufacturer. Since many sprays are highly poisonous they should be locked away from access by children and any unauthorised person.

Spray early in the morning on a calm day when no rain is expected for twenty-four hours. An early start allows the job to be completed before family and friends start wandering about. Otherwise, they may be offended by hearing a muffled snarl from behind a mask telling them to clear off. Protective clothing should be used and also rubber gloves, particularly when mixing sprays and cleaning equipment. A half mask respirator costing about $20 is a good investment. These are available from industrial protection companies who will advise on the correct type of filter cartridges to use. I recommend a RQ2000 respirator with RC86 cartridges. A respirator

A container of sundews with an orange background offers a one-way trip to whitefly and other insects. Environmentally friendly and on duty twenty-four hours a day—they are good members of the hydroponic team.

should always be used when spraying in the confined space of a polyhouse and spraying should start from the end furthest from the door. You should then back towards the other end and the exit. The professionals use more expensive positive pressure respirators which give complete protection against the inhalation of chemical sprays.

HYDROHINT

Devise a plan to keep pests away from your hydroponic plants and stick to it. If a problem develops, deal with it promptly. Even hosing a plant down as a temporary measure is a positive action.

CHAPTER 9

Getting Started

This chapter contains information on the weight and prices of mediums and some practical comments which may help the reader to select an economically acceptable and physically manageable approach to hydroponics. Please note carefully the hydrohints. Let's now get down to business and start some hydroponic growth!

Basic Equipment

First obtain your medium (see Chapter 3). Ideally this can be done by knowing a hydroponics enthusiast, as most of them will fall over backwards to encourage a potential convert. If you are lucky, a local hydroponics society or supplier may let you have a small quantity. Let's suppose you can obtain a 9 litre (2.3 US gal) laundry bucket of one of the following, and then we will put it to use.

Scoria

This is particularly easy to obtain in Victoria and a bucketful usually costs less than a dollar. Middle-sized particles (about 1 cm (2/5 in) in diameter) are best. A bucket full of the dry material weighs some 8 kg (18 lb) and so it's not something you want to carry too far. The wet scoria weighs only about 500 g (1 lb 1 1/2 oz) more than the dry material, but this does not take into account weight loss due to removal of the fine particles of dust. For tips on how to remove this dust, see Chapter 3.

Perlite

Perlite is available from most nurseries, but unfortunately the packets they sell are usually small and expensive. My local nursery sells small bags of about 8 litres (2 US gal) for A$6 which seems ridiculous when one considers that a 100 litres (26.2 US gal) bag of perlite granules costs about A$25 at the larger outlets. Nine litres (2.3 US gal) of dry perlite weighs only about 1 kg (2 lb 3 oz) but when wet its weight increases to 4 kg (8 lb 14 oz). As mentioned in Chapter 3, perlite should be moistened before handling as the dry material may be harmful if inhaled.

Vermiculite

Vermiculite is available from most garden suppliers but, as with perlite, small packets are very expensive. A 100 litres (26.2 US gal) bag of vermiculite costs about A$25. As described on page 19, it is usually used in combination with perlite to produce an excellent all-round medium.

Expanded Clay

Most of the larger hydroponic retailers sell 50 litre (13 US gal) bags of pH-stable European grade clay balls, costing around A$40.

A Growool Slab

These measure 75 x 31 x 80 cm (30 x 12 x 33 in) and are sold in packs of eight for about A$38, or singly at A$5.50. A dry slab weighs 2 kg (4 lb 6 oz); when saturated and drained its weight increases to 8 kg (17 lb 10 oz). Wrapped individual slabs of growool are also available (see the photograph on page 21). These are sealed in plastic and two square windows are cut out of the upper surface providing room for planting; the remaining covering acts as a delicate container. The wrapped slabs may be bought singly for about A$7 or in packs of eight for A$52.

Granulated Growool

Granulated growool is available in bags of 12.5 kg (27 lb 8 oz) which cost about A$20. This is a good investment for the home hydroponicer. A packed 9 litre (2.3 US gal) bucket of this medium weighs 1.5 kg (3 lb 5 oz) when dry and a hefty 6.3 kg (14 lb) when wet.

If you cannot obtain scoria or any of the other mediums mentioned, then you could use well washed river sand or stone screenings, but these are not really recommended for small-scale hydroponics. Sawdust is also a possibility.

Nutrients

Next obtain some ready mixed nutrients, but make sure they are clearly labelled as suitable for hydroponics. Most middle-sized nurseries stock a range of hydroponic nutrients and the major manufacturers and outlets are listed in the Appendix.

What quantity should you buy? As a general rule, the smaller the pack, the greater the relative cost of the contents. This applies to both powders and liquid nutrients. A container of 250 gm (9 oz) of nutrient might cost A$6 whereas the same preparation in a 1 kg bag might sell for A$13.

Frankly, I think a beginner is better off with a plentiful supply of nutrient rather than having to eke out a small quantity. Should you abandon hydroponics the remainder can be used as a true complete plant food. Incidentally, some hydroponic societies make bulk purchases so they can provide their members or potential members with low priced nutrients.

As far as I know there are as yet no tableted nutrients manufactured in Australia which are suitable for hydroponics. For some years, Dr Graeme Blackman and I have been endeavouring to produce cheap hydroponic tablets particularly for use in small hydroponic units. We have successfully developed tablets, which are very conve-nient — one tablet is used per litre of water to produce half-strength nutrient solution. They have proved ideal for beginners but unfortunately the cost of manufacture using the optimal formulation makes them too expensive to be commercially viable. This is a pity, as my late mother found the tablets wonderfully easy to use. Being nearly blind it was much easier for her to drop a tablet into the container of water than calculate the proverbial 'level teaspoon'. Dr Blackman and I will keep the possibility of manufacturing this useful tablet under review.

Non-recycling Systems

You are now ready to attempt some simple non-recycling systems. You can put them practically anywhere out-of-doors as any excess nutrient solution will drain out of the containers onto your patio or garden. The solution usually does not cause any staining of concrete, etc., and it is non-toxic — in fact my cats are quite partial to the occasional drink of nutrient solution.

A Small Herb Garden

A visit to the local supermarket led to the discovery of some excellent containers reduced to a mere 98 cents. I bought a few so that a variety of mediums could be used and the results compared.

The photographs on page 102 show the materials and plants needed for a herb garden, using perlite as the medium. Chives, parsley and thyme are a good combination because they have a long and productive life and don't take over each other's territory, as does mint, for example, which is best grown in its own container.

Cover the drainage holes in the container with some non-metallic gauze and, after spraying water lightly into the bag of perlite (see Chapter 3), fill the container with dampened perlite. Then remove the thyme and parsley plants from the pots and wash the soil or other material from their roots. Insert the plants into the perlite to the same depth that they previously occupied in their pots. Next sprinkle chive seeds over a section of the perlite at a rate of about one seed per 2 square centimetres

(0.3 sq in). The seeds should be covered with a sprinkling of additional perlite, just enough to cover them. Lightly water the container and protect it from direct sunlight for four or five days. It should not be left in a cold place as germination of the seeds is best encouraged if the temperature is between 18 and 22°C (64 and 74°F).

The container should be watered daily with water alone until about the fifth day when little chive shoots become visible and feeding with half-strength nutrient can begin. In mild weather nutrient solution will be needed either daily or every second day, but twice daily feeding may be necessary in hot weather. During heat wave conditions protect the herbs by putting them in the shade. Some people set up two herb gardens at once and alternate them between the kitchen and a sunny position.

If you mix up, say, 8 litres (2.1 US gal) of dilute nutrient at a time this should be adequate for a week. Every two months apply water only for several days to flush out any mineral excess which may have built up. In time, these very rewarding herb gardens usually grow a layer of moss over the surface. This does the herbs little harm and is quite attractive. However, it may for example restrict the growth of chives and should be peeled back from their territory.

Growool

I chose perlite for this venture because of its ready availability. Personally I prefer granulated growool or shaped growool slabs for herbs because the greater moisture retention of these mediums allows the herbs to survive for days or even weeks if feeding has been neglected.

With growool the same procedure is adopted as with perlite, except it must be dampened thoroughly with half-strength nutrient solution when in the container before planting. Plant the thyme and parsley as above and deposit the chive seeds on the surface of the growool. If you have some perlite available, it is helpful to sprinkle a little over the chive seeds. If you can't protect them a little from light by this method, then take especial care to keep the container away from direct sunlight and cover it with paper during the germination period.

A SMALL HERB GARDEN

A What you will need: herbs, a container, chive seeds, nutrient mixture, a bag of perlite and a watering can.

B A container of perlite set up as a herb garden — if you look very carefully the sprinkled chive seeds can be seen.

C Ten weeks later the container is packed with herbs and regular harvesting can begin.

Scoria

Scoria supports herbs well and makes an attractive base for their growth. Preparation and planting is the same as for perlite.

Should disaster strike your herb garden due to excessive heat or absent-minded neglect and all the plants appear to have expired, try watering it regularly for a few days. You can remember to do this by placing it near the kitchen sink. You may be amazed at the ability of herbs to recover from a near fatal experience.

Don't forget that the more vigorously you harvest the herbs the faster will be the growth of fresh flavoursome foliage.

Incidentally, these little herb gardens make excellent gifts for friends. You need only give them the established garden with instructions from you and some 100 g (3 1/2 oz) of your nutrient in a jar. All my friends have been well pleased with the results — but do cast an expert eye over your gift when you visit, as most people do not cut back the growth regularly enough.

Silver Beet

Take a clean 15 cm (6 in) plastic plant pot and, to stop the medium escaping, place some nylon flywire mesh or shadecloth inside it to cover the holes. Any other non-metallic mesh or gauze can be used — even old Wettex cloth. Now fill the pot

SILVERBEET

A Three containers and the shadecloth.

B Silverbeet seedlings removed from the growing trays, showing the wedge-shaped root formation.

C Seedlings planted.

D Silverbeet at eight weeks ready to provide the first meal.

with the selected medium and thoroughly dampen it with fresh water from a watering can.

This sized pot is a bit too small for a tomato plant but adequate for, say, capsicum or silver beet. The latter is a good plant for the beginner so we will start with some six-week-old silver beet which in the example are the colourful Swiss chard species. The seedlings can be raised in your garden or bought in. The second photograph shows the plants after removal from their seedling tray. When planting in scoria, I don't always wash the seed-raising mixture away from the plant's roots prior to planting, as it protects them from damage when the abrasive scoria is packed around the root system. The seed-germinating mixture is soon washed out by successive applications of nutrient solution.

When planting is complete the nutrient solution should be prepared at half-strength. The plant will need only about 200 ml (6 fl oz) a day, but when it has reached the same height as the pot or when the weather is hot it should be fed twice a day. About six weeks after planting you can start harvesting the leaves (see Chapter 6) and this can continue at weekly or fortnightly intervals for eighteen months or more.

In very hot weather it may be advisable to cover a black pot planter with some white material to prevent it becoming too hot. Alternatively, you can select a light coloured pot planter at the outset.

This simple plant pot unit can be converted to a recycling system by placing a wide but shallow bowl under the container to collect the nutrient solution which can later be poured back over the medium. A shallow bowl is best, because we want the solution to be drained out and not waterlog the medium. Fresh water will have to be added from time to time to the collected solution to keep the nutrients from becoming too concentrated. The nutrient solution should be replaced every ten to fourteen days.

Using a Growool Slab

As described earlier in the chapter a saturated whole growool slab weighs at least 8 kg (17 lb 10 oz) so most people will prefer to leave it and the plants growing in it on the one site.

GROWING EGGPLANTS IN GROWOOL SLABS

A The growool slab is cut into smaller blocks with a sharp knife (nothing blunts a knife like growool, so resharpening will be necessary before it goes back to the kitchen).

B The growool block is thoroughly saturated in water for at least ten minutes; it can then be taken out and drained.

C Eggplant seedlings are carefully removed from their growing trays.

<u>D</u> The seed-growing medium is gently washed under running water to reveal the delicate root network.

<u>E</u> A suitable opening is made in the growool slab.

<u>F</u> The plant is then inserted in the block and growool firmed up around it.

<u>G</u> The growool block introduced to the hydroponic system.

<u>H</u> The block is covered with white plastic for protection against light.

You need not use the whole slab in the one system. For example, you can slice off a strip about 10 cm (4 in) wide with a sharp knife and use this block for growing chives as described in Chapter 6. The block can be trimmed to fit, say, a plastic ice-cream tray. Remember to make holes for drainage.

A growool slab requires firm support. A common way of doing this is to encase the slab in plastic and rest it on slightly sloping ground. If the slab is being set up on a patio or concrete, a little sand or a board can be placed on one side to produce the few degrees of slope required. Three large drainage holes should be made in the plastic near the lowest edge of the slab. Expose the upper surface of the slab by cutting away a large rectangle of plastic. By using plastic in this way you reduce loss of moisture and promote drainage in the one direction. Opaque plastic sheeting is ideal for wrapping the slabs since it insulates them and discourages the growth of algae.

A large plastic tray also makes a good support, but it will need drainage holes made in it. Usually it is hard to find a tray which is big enough for a full slab.

Once the slab is in position and has been saturated with half-strength nutrient solution, planting may be carried out. This is done exactly as described with other mediums, taking care not to plant too deeply since this medium can hold so much moisture that there is more danger of the plants becoming waterlogged than with other mediums. If seedlings have been started in the

---

USING WHOLE GROWOOL SLABS

<u>A</u> The authors prepared a growool slab on a sloping stainless steel tray and placed it in the site where it was to be used. It was thoroughly soaked using a garden hose before connecting it to the hydroponic system.

<u>B</u> The growool slab was then covered with white plastic and holes cut in it for the insertion of plants just like the eggplant photographs on pages 104 and 105.

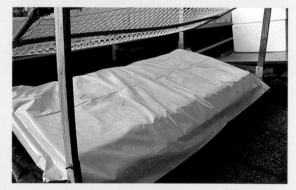

<u>C</u> Miniature roses in a similar growool slab.

smaller growool cubes or blocks, they can be placed directly on top of the slab, which will be quickly penetrated by their roots. Most plants grow on these slabs, with the exception of those like carrots, parsnips and potatoes which require considerable depth for their roots.

For starters you could try lettuces or silver beet, say a total of six plants to a whole block. Two tomato plants or a few capsicums are other good choices.

Feeding the right amount of nutrient solution to the growool block is easy if the block is well drained. In mild weather 5 litres (1.3 US gal) of half-strength nutrient every four days should be quite adequate until the plants are half mature, when they may need feeding every second day. In hot weather, especially with mature plants, feeding should be done daily. Always use half-strength nutrient solution. Every two months the slab should be well watered with fresh water to remove any mineral build-up.

Experienced hydroponicers lay the blocks level not sloping and feed carefully predetermined quantities of solution which keep the medium moist but not saturated. The medium, of course, gradually dries up through exposure to the air. The amateur may succeed with this approach but usually only after he or she has gained considerable experience. It is safer to stick to a well-drained, frequently-saturated medium.

Recycling Systems

1 Tomato, Capsicum and Sweet William in a Plastic Laundry Bucket

We are going to grow a Gross Lisse tomato, a capsicum and, for a bit of colour, a dwarf Sweet William. These will grow in harmony and to different heights. Regardless of the medium used, you will need the following: a 9 litre (2.3 US gal) laundry bucket, a 20 cm (8 in) square piece of nylon flywire screen or sunshade material to act as a filter, a length of hose or rubber tube about 60 cm (24 in) long and a 5 litre (1.3 US gal) plastic watering can. A 1.2 metre (4 ft) stake to support the tomato plant will also be required unless you

are going to position the unit next to a wall or some other source of support. A timber stake will do quite well but a cleaner choice is the length of plastic pipe seen in the photographs.

First we have to make an outlet 4 cm (1 1/2 in) above the bottom of the bucket to which we will attach the hose. The best way to do this is to drill a hole and cut a thread which will take a screw-in plastic outlet (see pages 26–8). However, since we are just starting off, it will be enough merely to make a hole big enough for us to squeeze 1 or 2 cm (2/5 or 4/5 in) of the hose into the bucket. You can do this with a drill or a soldering iron which you can borrow if you don't have one yourself. If the fit is not perfect a good seal can be made using a silicone sealant or teflon tape. Fitting the hose is the only technical job in this hydroponic venture.

Next the material to be used as a filter is folded double and placed over the hose outlet inside the bucket, the stake is positioned at the rear of the bucket and the bucket is filled with the selected medium (granulated growool, perlite or scoria). Then take the three plants, which should all be six weeks old, gently wash the seed-germinating mixture off them (Chapter 5) and gently plant them in the medium to the same depth as in their original pots. The tomato goes to the rear next to the stake, the capsicum in the middle and the Sweet William to the front. If using scoria, which is quite abrasive material, be particularly gentle when settling it around the plants.

If the weather is very hot at the time of planting it is best to keep the plants out of the sun for several days while they are becoming established. After this the bucket can be placed in a sunny area sheltered from wind, and it should be elevated about 40 cm (16 in) or so off the ground.

As soon as the planting has been done the first feeding can be carried out. Mark the 4 litre (1 US gal) level on the watering can and make up this volume of nutrient solution but make it one-half the strength recommended by the manufacturer. The solution is poured into the bucket from the watering can, keeping the outlet end of the hose elevated so that the nutrient solution thoroughly saturates the medium. After a minute or so the hose can be lowered to drain the bucket either

TOMATOES AND CAPSICUMS IN BUCKETS

<u>B</u> Close-up of plants in scoria.

<u>A</u> Tomato and basil plants growing in buckets. The mediums used are scoria, perlite and granulated growool.

<u>C</u> The same plants seven weeks later. This rapid growth occurred in the igloo. They were taken outside briefly for this photograph.

back into the watering can or into some other container. This flood and drain procedure should be repeated daily in milder weather but carried out twice a day when the weather is hot and/or the plants are growing quickly. You will notice that the volume of liquid returned to the watering can starts diminishing after a day or so due to the plants' thirst and evaporation. It is essential to top the level up to the 4 litre (1 US gal) mark in the watering can with fresh water otherwise the nutrient concentration will significantly increase and harm the plants.

Usually, in these little systems, gardeners discard the nutrient solution every seven or ten days and prepare a new one. Pour the old nutrient onto some deserving pot plant, which will probably show its appreciation.

After about a month you can start using full-strength nutrient solution, but only do this if you are sure you will remember to maintain the right water level in the watering can. Every six weeks flush the bucket out with fresh water to remove any mineral build-up.

Keep a close eye open for any insect pests or diseases (Chapter 8), and don't forget to remove the lower laterals from the tomato as described in Chapter 6. At the end of the season the tomato plant can be gently pulled out. The capsicum may go on for another year and the Sweet William will probably flower away busily for as long as it is fed.

Next year a new tomato plant can replace its predecessor.

It may seem a bit of a chore having to attend to this unit once or twice a day, but it soon proves very rewarding. If you have to go away for a few days and can't find anyone to look after it, just feed it and leave it in the bathroom until you return. It will probably understand and continue to flourish when moved outside again.

Some examples of this simple bucket recycling system can be seen in the photographs.

2 A Carrot Box

A regular supply of carrots can easily be obtained by growing them in a 28 cm (11in) container filled to a depth of 20 cm (8 in) with perlite. You will need a plastic container (say 30 by 40 cm (12 by 16 in) for a family of four), perlite, 50 cm (20 in) of hose or tubing, a 9 litre (2.3 US gal) watering can with the 4 litre (1 US gal) level marked as in the previous example, nutrient, water and a packet of carrot seeds. Any sort of carrots do well, so just select a type that appeals to you. However, the very long species prefer a container depth of some 30 cm (12 in).

If you want to be more certain of success it is a good idea to add some vermiculite, say one part in four, to the perlite. This increases the water-holding capacity of the media which is a great advantage to the plants, particularly if you forget or are going away and are unable to water them for a few days. A little vermiculite, particularly on the surface, maintains a better moisture level for germination.

Make a hole 4 cm (1 1/2 in) from the bottom of the container, cover it with gauze on the inside, and insert the hose from the outside (see previous example). Now put the container on a bench or platform in a sunny position and raise the side opposite the hole so the hose or tube drains to the watering can beneath it. Obviously you will have to make sure the container is higher than the watering can or other collecting vessel. Now fill the box with dampened perlite (see Chapter 3), sprinkle the carrot seeds on the surface, and very lightly cover them with more perlite or vermiculite.

A CARROT BOX

A Young carrots growing in perlite/vermiculite mixture.

B The harvest; seeds can be sown immediately.

(*Note:* we have filled the container after it is in its final position rather than trying to lift it when it is filled with dampened perlite. Best to avoid back strain.)

Each day gently water the container using a watering can with a fine rose. After a week or so, tiny shoots should have appeared. Keep the container covered with, say, a board during this period.

Now fill the watering can with half-strength solution and water the carrots, keeping the draining hose elevated so the media is well flooded. After a few minutes, allow the contents to drain back into the watering can or other container.

HYDROHINTS

Do

* Start on a very small scale to get the feel of hydroponics.
* Join a hydroponics society and see as many amateur and professional setups as possible.
* Visit the hydroponic display at Garden Week exhibitions.
* Contact your State Agriculture Department for advice and information.
* Consider doing a course in hydroponics. A range of these is offered by some tertiary colleges or adult education centres (see Appendix).
* Read as many books on hydroponics as you can lay your hands on. Every author has some views which differ from others. The discerning reader can pick up some useful new hints from practically any hydroponics book.

Don't

* Rush off and buy a glasshouse and/or expensive equipment. Take your time and decide exactly what will suit your needs and capabilities.
* Give up if you have a failure. It will not be the fault of the plant. If you cannot decide what went wrong, seek advice.
* Attempt to become dependent upon hydroponics for a living unless you can prove beyond doubt that in your case and position the proposition is viable.
* Construct large concrete beds or tanks unless you have considerable expertise, otherwise you may have to live with an ugly, malfunctioning and immovable structure.

Repeat the process daily, except in very hot weather when you should water twice a day.

Always water using the rose because, if you pour a lot of nutrient in suddenly, the carrots may be overexposed. Also the sudden pooling of liquid may cause the finer perlite particles to sediment and block the outlet.

The level in the watering can should be topped up with water regularly to keep the nutrient solution from becoming too strong. The solution should be replaced every fortnight. Every two months flush the container out by using water only in the watering can.

Young carrots can be harvested at any time. You just need to wipe off any adhering perlite and they can be eaten on the spot. Most people thin them out, using the smaller ones for salads and leaving the others to increase in size. Reseeding can be done any time. The best way to do this is to clear, say, one-third of the carrots and spread the seeds in this area. Remember to use water without nutrient solution on the reseeding area until the shoots have appeared and, if possible, keep it covered.

Later, the next one-third can be resown and so on. In this way a constant supply of carrots of various ages will be available.

I have not tried growing carrots in either scoria or growool. Other hydroponicers have had some success using scoria or sand, but I have found perlite so satisfactory there has been no motivation to try alternatives. A carrot box filled with perlite is a sound investment.

A carrot box connected up to a recycling system driven by an electric pump is an automatic carrot producer and I wouldn't be without one.

3 Using a Submersible Electric Pump

Don't do anything hasty. If you have a sales outlet for this equipment nearby, then leave your cheque book or credit cards at home and go and inspect what is available. Best of all, visit the gardens of any successful amateurs in your neighbourhood. You can perhaps get their names from your nearest hydroponic society. You need to determine which is the best priced and most reliable pump as well as accessibility to after sales service. Furthermore, the pump must be selected to suit the dimensions of your proposed hydroponic system.

Buying a kit with a submersible pump

You can of course by-pass the obstacles of pump selection by purchasing a manufactured kit already complete with an electric pump. It is strongly advised that care be taken with such a purchase as a few are of dubious value and/or unattractive. Of late, many retailers have been able to stock good kits, particularly flood and drain types (see pages 38–9). If you can afford it, a small reliable kit is an excellent way to get into hydroponics.

I do not propose to go into details concerning the setting up of this type of recycling system, since they are best studied at first-hand and can be arranged in a variety of ways to suit each hydroponicer's needs. A picture of a very simple installation may be helpful. This system shows a submersible electric pump in the bottom of a tank and a ball valve to replenish the tank with fresh water. The pump feeds the nutrient solution via drippers to plants growing in perlite. The returned nutrient is strained through a simple open filter. All the fittings including all-plastic ball valves are available from normal plumbing suppliers.

The happy hydroponicer – the author's system at work

After four years of working in a small glasshouse and having a variety of hydroponic systems meandering across the garden, it was decided to set up a large polyhouse (or igloo) and make the whole system as automatic as possible. Costs were to be kept well under A$1 000 and, most important, the unit would have to be attractive and in no way annoy the neighbours. Furthermore, it had to be classified as a temporary or removable structure because of council regulations. In order to make room for it, a derelict laundry had to be removed along with the kids' playhouse and, although the latter is missed for sentimental reasons, the whole family seems both proud and pleased with the igloo. Apart from hydroponic pursuits, it is a fine spot for morning or afternoon tea or even for a quiet read. On a winter's day, when the sunshine is weak, the interior is warm and free from biting wind and so it fulfils an additional role as the family sunroom. It is also a good studio for the amateur painter.

The igloo has been up now for ten years. We have certainly had our money's worth from it and wonder how on earth we got on without one before. It allows instant escape from Melbourne weather!

Speaking of money, costs of hydroponic equipment, etc., have not increased greatly in recent

years. This may be because of greater demand, larger production runs and increased competition. This observation should encourage the beginner!

Establishing the Hydroponic Environment

The igloo was set up on flat ground 1 metre (3 ft 3 in) from the rear fence and running lengthwise east–west. The one chosen measured 7.6 by 4.5 metres (24 ft 11 in by 14 ft 9 in). It consists of a frame made of galvanised piping with arches every 1.5 metres (4 ft 11 in). There are many types of plastic covers available, including those with built-in air bubbles for insulation. Heavy gauge ultraviolet-light stabilised polyfilm was recommended by the manufacturer, since its price was low and life expectancy in the proposed situation probably over three years.

In fact, almost three years to the day cracking developed in this polyfilm and a new cover was urgently required. It split in mid-winter. The whole area looked like a disaster zone and depressed everyone. I was advised to get a Solarweave cover. I blanched at the price (over A$200) but the choice was in fact brilliant. It looks lovely and at the time of writing is still intact eight years after being put in place. The

only holes in it are small and these were made by a demolition contractor who lit a huge bonfire next door to dispose of a stack of timber. The proud owner came home to find fireworks raining down from above onto his new Solarweave cover. It was not a time to mince words, the fire was extinguished and the damage repaired with silicone sealant. However, there are now a number of other types of long-life covers available and it may pay the reader to visit one of the factories which fabricate tailor-made covers so they can select the most appropriate one for their needs. (See Appendix.)

The original igloo manufacturer offered an assembly service and this was accepted with the proviso of a modification, namely the raising of the whole unit 60 cm (24 in) off the ground with additional vertical piping. This was quite cheap and allowed much better use of the interior. Taller plants could be grown and it was possible to walk around near the walls without stooping.

At each end I installed plastic flaps 1.8 by 1.8 metres (5 ft 11 in by 5 ft 11 in) supported by three wooden battens. The flaps could be rolled up to provide ventilation. A number of laundry taps were left standing forlornly in one corner and so, for a 'few extra bob', the man who assembled the unit connected one up to three misting outlets placed along the central roof support using heavy

Picture of the author's garden. The Solarweave cover on the igloo is now ten years old. The tomato shed is seen on the left.

hose. I never regret this small expense, especially in hot weather. Later I bought a balance arm mister activator and this meant that when at work during a heatwave I knew that the misting system would be automatically turning itself on and off, keeping the plants cool and moist. This simple and reliable device was made by Sage Horticultural (see Appendix) but other types of cut-off devices are available.

I now had a veritable barn professionally erected and thereafter, apart from an electrician, could manage without skilled help. After my glasshouse it looked so huge inside I had some doubts as to whether I had overestimated my requirements. A year later I was wishing space was available to extend it!

I spread several centimetres (or inches) of coarse sand over the ground inside and then stretched one continuous sheet of black woven plastic anti-weed cloth over the sand and fixed it

to all the edges with wooden battens. Next, insect-proofing was carried out using shadecloth. One entrance was sealed with this material and, at the other end, a sliding door with an aluminium frame was fitted and counterweighed so it closed automatically. The door and its surrounds were covered with shadecloth.

Setting up the Hydroponic Plumbing

Plumbing suppliers are like an Alladin's cave to the hydroponicer. Such a huge selection of easily fitted plastic pipes, elbows and other accessories allows cheap construction of an attractive system to suit precisely a particular situation. Commercial and domestic dripper or sprinkling equipment outlets also have a wide range of items to select from. The staff are usually very helpful and often encyclopaedic in their knowledge.

Incidentally, the names of many plumbers' items have a Chaucerian ring to them which may at first embarrass the unworldly. However, it's worth

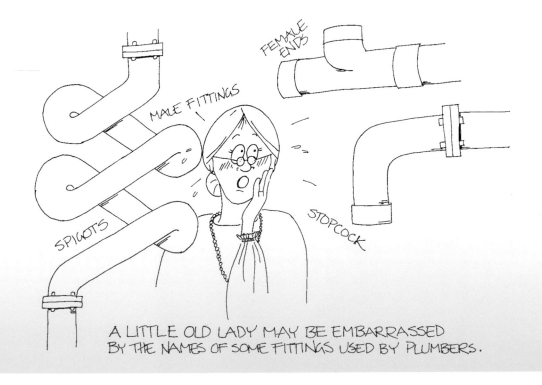

FEMALE ENDS

MALE FITTINGS

SPIGOTS

STOPCOCK

A LITTLE OLD LADY MAY BE EMBARRASSED BY THE NAMES OF SOME FITTINGS USED BY PLUMBERS.

learning a little plumbing language since it can be used with effect on appropriate occasions.

I wanted a flexible system so that I could make improvements as I gained experience. To give rigid support to the benches I used steel star posts driven into the ground through a neat cut in the plastic flooring. When necessary, these were easily removed and the small break in the flooring repaired with a patch and adhesive. Using cross-pieces of treated pine or other steel posts I rapidly constructed quite solid structures. After a brush down with mineral turpentine, the steel posts were given two coats of green enamel paint seven days apart. The effect was quite pleasing.

Nutrient Reservoir

I estimated that a reservoir of about 300 litres (79 US gal) of nutrient would be adequate to supply the plants. After visiting a few factories, I was given two heavy 'non-returnable' black plastic drums of 200 litres (53 US gal) capacity. These had screw-top lids 30 cm (12 in) in diameter. After careful cleaning the two were connected low down by 5 cm (1 1/2 in) piping which was sealed with a silicone preparation (see the diagram). A small float valve was fitted halfway down one tank and a hose fitting attached to its exterior outlet so that there would be an inflow of fresh tap water when the nutrient level fell and opened the valve. The double tank was then lowered into a hole some 60 cm (24 in) below ground level immediately outside the rear end of the igloo.

Selection and Installation of the Electric Pump

A variety of submersible corrosive-resistant electric pumps designed for garden fountains were tested but all were inadequate because they could not raise a sufficient level of water over 1.8 metres (5 ft 11 in). As outlined below, there are a number of significant advantages in being able to raise the nutrient solution to this height. Smaller units will, of course, function quite well on a lower level.

Over the years a succession of pumps have been

THE HEART OF A HYDROPONIC SYSTEM

A The heart of the hydroponic system, an electric swimming pool pump.

B View of the pumping system and nutrient reservoirs from above.

C When connected, this mercury float switch will cut the electric motor if nutrient level falls too low. A very sound investment! This pump control is one of a number manufactured by S. J. Electro Systems and is available from many swimming pool pump distributors in Australia.

used. The most reliable set-up has been with an Australian-made Onga pump, model 413, combined with a mercury float-switch which cuts off power to the pump when the reservoir reaches a pre-determined level (see the photograph on page 115). The model JSD is not sensitive to rotation but is effected by turbulence so it was installed in the return nutrient tank where it has functioned perfectly. S. J. Electro Systems also manufacture pumps which tolerate turbulence but these are more expensive. The importance of a safety cut-out cannot be overstressed as it eliminates the risk of the pump running dry and burning out. Incidentally, this Onga pump and others like it are very business-like.

It is possible to connect the hydroponic garden directly to the pump instead of using an elevated tank but, because of the high output, a large proportion of the nutrient will be directed straight back to the tank it has just come from. This does no harm and helps aerate the nutrient solution.

The foot valve and other fittings necessary to keep the pump primed are standard items sold by swimming pool shops. Indeed the improvement in swimming pool pumps and filtration equipment is another benefit for the hydroponicer. Power to the electric motor is activated by a time switch at intervals as outlined in Chapter 7, page 83.

There are some large imported submersible pumps of high output which have float-operated switches. This float cuts the power off when the level becomes low. My experience was that the float had a tendency to detach itself and not fulfil its function. After the second pump burnt out due to float failure, it was the end for me and I went back to the non-submersible pump with foot valve and reliable float-switch as described above.

Power Supply

Ideally a permanent waterproof power supply should have been installed, but quotes from several electricians appeared more fitting to a goldmine than a suburban hydroponic unit. On the other hand, it was out of the question for reasons both of safety and appearance to have a normal extension cord snaking its way from the house, across the garden to the unit. I solved the problem by getting an electrician to install an exterior power point with a safety cut-out device at the nearest corner of the house. He then tailor-made a heavy-duty power cable which ran from the power point along the fence and into the igloo where it entered underneath a small wooden bedside cabinet which had been rescued from the local tip. Inside the cabinet it was connected to a multiple power outlet. Additional 5 cm (2 in) holes were made in the bottom of the cabinet for the entry leads to the power outlet. This arrangement assured that all connections were made in an elevated and dry area. The cabinet also stored small tools, ties and bits and pieces such as labels and marking pens. A coat of white paint made it the focal point, a position it had not enjoyed since it housed a potty many years earlier.

After a year of so the humidity in the igloo caused signs of disintegration to appear and so the wooden cabinet was replaced by a large plastic box which was raised 2 metres (6 ft 7 in) off the ground. This satisfactorily kept all electrical connections free from moisture.

Path of the Nutrient Solution
(see diagram)

Earlier editions of this book described a rather complicated set-up which involved elevated overflow tanks. The current system is simpler and has proven more reliable. The nutrient solution is drawn with vigour from the pump tank and has a choice of two pathways after leaving the pump. Most of the fluid takes the first option which is to return to the pump tank where mixing and good aeration takes place. The remainder of the nutrient solution passes into the igloo where it flows through multiple links of 13 mm (1/2 in) black plastic tubing which radiate out to a variety of containers. The blind ends of the plastic tubing are either fitted with small taps or folded over and firmly taped. This allows occasional flushing out of all lines.

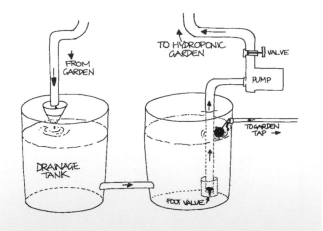

Path of the nutrient solution from the two connected drainage tanks.

HYDROHINT
Make sure the pump for the nutrient solution is adequate for your needs.

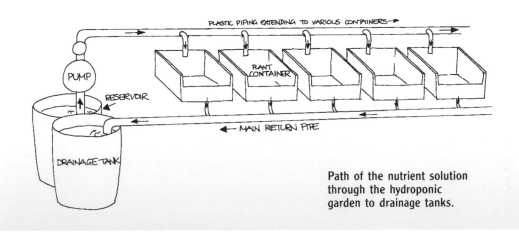

Path of the nutrient solution through the hydroponic garden to drainage tanks.

Mixed flowers growing in growool.

Returning nutrients are filtered through aquarium wool and a kitchen sieve.

Interior of the igloo in late winter. Part of the white 'U'-shaped main drainage pipe can be clearly seen.

Many of the drippers are inserted directly into the tubing and others via narrower extensions. It is a time-consuming business to make sure fittings are tight, the drippers accessible for cleaning and that everything is as neat as possible. The average number of drippers used is about sixty. All are Turbo-Key drippers and the various types all give a similar performance. However, the simpler variable flow dripper is the easiest to clean.

Nutrient Drainage (Return) Pipe

The pipe draining the nutrient had to be of wide bore to cope with the flow as well as to prevent blockage. Plastic downpiping, 50 mm (2 in) in diameter, proved ideal. A 'U' shape of piping was made to run the length of the igloo with a cross-piece near the rear end. It was attached to steel posts about 30 cm (12 in) from the ground and

sloped gently towards the rear. A short extension carried the nutrient into the top of the drainage tank. Directly under the outlet of this pipe a plastic basket filled with aquarium wool was positioned as a filter for the circulating nutrient.

Containers and Mediums Used

I used both shallow and deep containers, depending upon plant and medium types. The shallowest containers consisted simply of growool slabs mounted on gently sloping metal trays which had been covered with plastic sheeting. The sheeting extended into plastic rainwater guttering which collected the nutrient solution and directed it towards the drainage system. Baguley polystyrene trays were also used as shallow containers. Lengths of guttering used as containers for growool or perlite gave a little more depth.

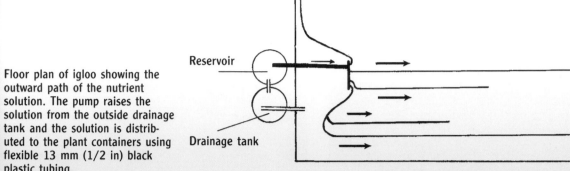

Floor plan of igloo showing the outward path of the nutrient solution. The pump raises the solution from the outside drainage tank and the solution is distributed to the plant containers using flexible 13 mm (1/2 in) black plastic tubing.

Reservoir

Drainage tank

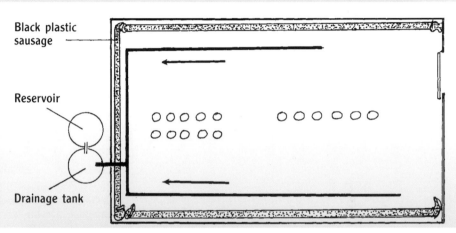

Floor plàn of igloo showing the position of the 'U'-shaped main drainage pipe which has a short extension to reach the outside drainage tank. Tiers of laundry buckets occupy the centre section and a variety of flat containers are on shelves which drain into the main drainage pipe below. On three sides of the igloo black plastic sausage tubing is laid on the floor and filled with water to act as a heat bank. Black plastic drums filled with water are placed under the plant containers as additional heat traps.

Black plastic sausage

Reservoir

Drainage tank

Interior of the igloo in early summer. Lush growth now fills every corner.

<u>A</u> The tiers of buckets are arranged so the nutrient drains into the second bucket below and then into the main drain. Another set of buckets is behind the long hydrotube against the plastic trellis.

<u>B</u> This second group of buckets is all on one level and drains initially into a length of flat plastic downpiping. On the left is an experimental planting of irises and redcurrants. The buckets can easily be moved around as the outlets are just sitting in the downpiping.

Plastic buckets (see Chapter 4) were my favourite deep containers. I purchased these in bulk when they were on special offer at sales. They had to be of good quality as the ones which tended to crack when squeezed also often cracked when holes were drilled for drainage outlets. The buckets were arranged in tiers or rows to maximise the use of space. Either perlite or granulated growool was used in the buckets. Other deep containers were old wooden laundry troughs lined with plastic and assorted plastic drums of up to 60 cm (24 in) in height. The largest containers I could find were used for the very big plants like bananas. The drainage outlets from the containers were covered with pieces of shadecloth to collect sludge and to hold back the perlite granules.

In recent years I have tended to use fewer plastic laundry buckets, replacing them with foam plastic boxes or larger plastic containers. The general rule is that if you are comfortable with what is available, use it. Some of the modern nutrient film technique kits are looking pretty tempting.

Several small tables for propagation trays, etc., were placed just inside the entrance so they could easily be attended to and observed regularly.

Nutrients Used

Various commercial nutrient mixtures and solutions designed specifically for hydroponics have been used and all those from the major manufacturers have proven satisfactory. One batch from a minor manufacturer which contained a lot of insoluble foreign material caused repeated chaos by blocking drippers. It took a while to cotton-on to this problem as the nutrient was being tipped straight into the reservoir where it disappeared from sight. I now stick to products which have well-known and respected brand names. There are many specialised nutrient combinations available but I stick quite happily to a standard local brew.

The preparation and replacement of the nutrient solution is discussed in Chapters 2 and 7.

Cooling and Ventilation of the Environment

On the first warm spring day it became obvious that by summer it was going to get very hot indeed inside the igloo. I didn't want to copy the commercial growers and slap a coat of paint over its exterior since that would look ugly as it weathered. Furthermore, I wanted to be able to vary the degree of protection according to the weather. The techniques used to protect the plants from excessive heat are outlined in Chapter 7 and the following describes my own sequence of developments.

As previously described, the back and front entrances were screened with shadecloth to exclude large insects when the plastic flaps at both ends were rolled up to increase air flow.

I then laid water-filled black plastic sausages around the edges of the igloo and placed as many black-painted or black plastic drums filled with water as could be found about the interior. These acted as heat banks (see Chapter 7).

Next, to reduce the heat of the afternoon sun, I painted a section of the roof and the north-eastern corner with flat plastic house paint using a roller on an extension rod. Some areas of polyfilm were left unpainted to act as windows but all the areas over the metal supports were painted. This was done because, by protecting the metal supports from extreme heat, the life of the polyfilm in contact with them would be extended. My paint had a faint blue tinge and the end result looked most attractive from the inside as the roller had made pleasant patterns not evident from outside.

I erected a plastic trellis in front of a portion of the sunniest aspect of the igloo and planted a grapevine and passionfruit there. These fast-growing plants gave good protection in summer but let in plenty of light during winter.

In spite of all these precautions the readings of a simple minimum–maximum recording thermometer made it clear that the internal temperature

> **HYDROHINT**
> Install the pump so that it is safe to use and fit it with a foolproof cut-out mechanism so it will not run dry and burn out.

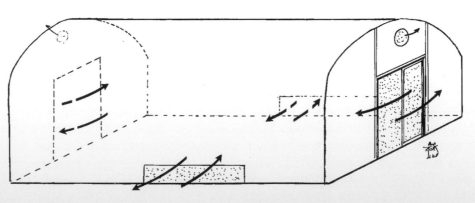

Air flow through the igloo. At each end the shadecloth measures 1.9 x 1.7 metres (6ft 3in x 5ft 7in) and the side vents are 3 x 0.6 metres (9ft 10in x 2ft). Good ventilation is essential for healthy plant growth.

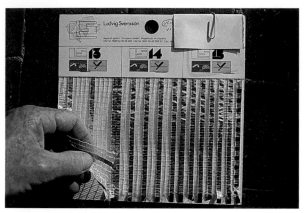

Samples of Ludvig Svensson screening materials which offer varying degrees of protection.

Thermostatically activated exhaust fans draw hot air from the igloo via ducting. In this photograph some of the screening can be seen: on the left lightweight Ludvig Svensson screening and on the other side green shade-cloth.

of the igloo could rise to over 40°C (104°F) whilst outside it was only about 25°C (77°F). Rather than paint more of the polyfilm, I made a cover of calico some 12 square metres (14.3 sq yd) with a dowelling rod threaded through each end. I attached thin nylon blind cords to the rods so that the cover could be pulled over the igloo in stages to give any desired degree of protection. When temperatures were forecast to be over 25°C (77°F) I simply pulled the cords to move the cover over the most exposed surface of the igloo. Later a further area of the roof was painted so that I only needed to use the cover on days when the forecast predicted temperatures greater than 35°C (95°F).

Inside the igloo I later used specially designed reflective woven aluminium cloth which is extraordinarily light and can be suspended by use of a fishing line and clothes pegs. Samples of this Swedish invention were provided by Living Shade. White shade-cloth also assisted greatly and eventually a white shadecloth external cover was purchased as it is light and long-lasting.

> **HYDROHINT**
> Without adequate ventilation, an igloo will overheat and become a death trap for plants. It is not too good for humans either!

The ventilation was still inadequate in very hot weather and so first one and, later, a second exhaust fan was installed. The simple ducting extracted air from the centre of the igloo (hot air rises!) and the electrician wired a thermostat so the fans would start up as soon as the temperature reached 30°C (86°F). The temperature probe was kept in a glass of water at head level in the igloo. The warming and cooling of the water resulted in a steadier operation of the cooling system.

Compact high extraction rate fans with slender ducting that are ideal for small igloos and glasshouses are now available. They cost several hundred dollars but this was about the cost of the two domestic fans that were originally installed. Greenlite, for example, stock these.

My misting system was only activated when the forecast temperatures were to be over 25°C (77°F) and it was set to mist for a minute or so about every 30 minutes during daylight.

Using these measures, internal temperature was very well controlled and heat stress to plants minimised. The temperature inside the igloo rarely exceeded the outside temperature and on very hot days with the intermittent misting the internal conditions were often more pleasant than outside.

The heat banks made the interior balmy at night when the outside was quite chilly. A temperature almost like tropical nights was produced if I lowered the plastic flaps at sunset. However, if I forgot to raise the flaps before going off to work next day there were some very sick half-baked plants at the end of the day.

All this about environment control may seem somewhat longwinded but, if one plans how to handle extremes of weather and adopt a simple routine, plant growth will be steady and healthy.

The Tomato Shed – a Purpose-built Unit

Near the igloo there was an eyesore, a little bit of land where nothing grew very well. Since the hydroponic pump and nutrient reservoir were more

THE TOMATO SHED

<u>A</u> The purpose-built tomato shed.

<u>B</u> Interior view of tomato shed.

<u>C</u> Proof of the pudding, Moonshot tomatoes being harvested.

than adequate for the igloo it was decided to build a simple hothouse, especially for growing tomatoes, since the igloo could not satisfy the demand.

The building had to be simple, cheap and extremely well ventilated as we now knew that over-heating was a terrible problem. The knowledge that hot air rises was going to be put to good advantage. To suit tomatoes it had to be narrow, but tall. A frame of treated pine was built 5 metres (16 ft 5 in) long, 1.8 metres (5 ft 11 in) wide and 2.2 metres (7 ft 2 in) high. The roof sloped slightly and, except for about 4 square metres (43 sq ft) of ventilation, the whole frame was encased in Solarweave. Staples and treated pine battens were used to fix the Solarweave. The ventilation panels were rendered largely insect-free using shadecloth. One of the largest vents was situated immediately below the roof so it allowed hot air to escape quickly. In summer, shadecloth frames were placed on the roof and rolls of shadecloth could cover the long western wall of the unit. A layer of sand was spread on the floor and then covered with anti-weed cloth. Setting up tomatoes in containers was child's play and the results have been excellent.

This unit was undoubtedly a 'good idea' and should be considered by any gardener as the dimensions can be tailored to suit the available area and cooling it does not pose problems nor should cost.

AN EXPERIMENT WITH ONIONS

<u>A</u> Eight-week-old onion plants growing hydroponically in perlite/vermiculite mixture.

<u>B</u> Onions that have been planted out in the garden for the same length of time (the weeds soon overcame them completely).

<u>C</u> Hydroponic onions being harvested three months later. One minuscule onion was the total yield from the garden bed.

Summary of Results

Chapter 6 deals with a broad range of plants which can successfully be grown hydroponically. The following is a synopsis of results obtained to date in the author's own system. The growing of many other plants is yet to be attempted and hopefully optimised. My commonest mistake was to overcrowd the plants, especially on growool slabs. Another was to start plants too early in the season or not realise that second plantings can do very well as late as towards the end of summer.

The prompt removal of aging or diseased plants requires a very positive attitude and I often failed to do this. I found that if I planned ahead and had the next occupant of a particular area ready, this provided sufficient impetus to remove the current tenant immediately it had fulfilled its purpose.

Asparagus

This has produced well and for a longer period than when grown in soil. It has been grown in plastic buckets with perlite as medium. As with carrots, I have always had great difficulty keeping an asparagus bed free of weeds when I have grown it in soil.

Bananas

Several of the Williams variety were grown as an experiment. They had to be removed from the igloo, because they grew so tall they threatened to lift it out of the ground. Hydroponic bananas are apparently grown with success in Iceland, but in Melbourne one would need a fairly high ceiling. They certainly enjoyed life in the igloo while it lasted.

Basil

Grown on growool slabs (or indeed any media) it often keeps going into winter if kept well pruned.

Beans (French)

At least three good crops have been grown per year equally well in all mediums used. However growool slabs or granulated growool gives the plants better support.

Beetroot

Does well on welldrained growool slabs or in perlite. Their growth seems a bit faster than in the garden and one avoids hours of weeding.

HYDROHINT

As a routine most commercial hydroponic establishments remove every single plant from a unit prior to careful cleaning and restocking. If possible, the amateur should try to follow this example.

Broccoli

Although the plants grow very quickly in any medium in buckets, I have obtained the best long-term results when they have been transferred to the garden when they were about 30 cm (12 in) high. The careful planting, feeding and regular spraying of such plants in soil seems to give better and longer harvests than other methods.

Capsicum

Does very well on growool slabs. With good pruning it may last several seasons.

Carnations (Sim)

Initially grown in perlite in Baguley trays, I now use growool slabs on sloping stainless steel trays. Although the fungal disease fusarium reduces their productivity and life expectancy, one gets many months of flower production and they must be considered a success.

Carrots

Excellent results obtained by sowing direct onto 20 cm (8 in) deep perlite. Regular planting ensures a year long supply.

Rosemary and thyme also grow well in plastic piping which has had a section removed, the medium is still perlite.

Horseradish growing in perlite. After harvesting, a few pieces of root are replaced and this becomes the second year's crop.

Celery

Fast growth has been regularly obtained using growool slabs. Quality is variable but it is quite suitable for cooking and flavouring.

Chives

Chives grow superbly on growool slabs, provided certain precautions are taken. The slabs have to be well drained and this was achieved by using sloping rainwater guttering. Experimentation found that the following led to complete germination of seeds and lush growth. A 10 by 40 cm (4 by 16 in) slab of growool was saturated with half-strength nutrient solution and then placed in the sloping guttering which was fed nutrient solution through the system. Chive seeds were sprinkled fairly densely on the growool. A packet will usually cover a 40 cm (16 in) length of guttering.

The seed was then lightly covered with a layer of perlite. Using this method and hand watering for five days the seeds are initially in contact with water only and the thin perlite can keep the emerging roots and shoots quite moist. In warm weather the chives will rise quickly through the perlite and by six weeks can be chopped back for kitchen use. By regularly and severely cutting them, a constant supply of fresh young shoots is guaranteed. Another reason for cutting them back is that the new growth is more disease-resistant.

Cucumber

Provided mildew-resistant strains are used, prolific crops follow the use of any medium.

Dahlias

The miniature variety has done splendidly in all mediums.

Garlic

Results have been excellent on well-drained growool slabs. Near maturity, when the leaves start yellowing, the slabs are allowed to dry out slowly to harden the garlic. The whole slab is then stored in a dry, dark but well-ventilated area and the garlic removed as required.

Herbs

Herbs like mint, parsley and thyme all grow well in plastic buckets filled with perlite.

Horseradish

Tender, mild horseradish grows effortlessly in plastic buckets of perlite. However, every six weeks or so its roots partially block the outlet of the bucket and have to be trimmed.

Leeks

A year round supply has been obtained, using either growool slabs or perlite. However, quite heavy saturation with nutrient solution is required for success with the latter medium.

Lettuces

To date in the igloo really good results have only been obtained in early summer. Probably the best reason for this is that lettuces were grown in positions which got too much direct sunlight later in the season which baked them on very hot days. The most consistent results have been obtained in the most sheltered corner of the igloo.

Lobelia

This grows magnificently in all mediums.

Marrows (Spaghetti)

To date the yield has been better out in the garden where these plants can rush off madly in all directions dropping new roots here and there as they go.

Potatoes growing in a double bucket system. The medium is granulated growool.

Parsnips

The best parsnips I have ever tasted were grown in perlite in a wooden laundry tub.

They were not only tender to the core but had a most pleasing fragrance. These were grown in a position of full sun which proved a failure with lettuces.

Potatoes

These are grown in a similar situation to the parsnips and do very well. One can slide a hand deep into the perlite and steal a couple of mature new potatoes from time to time without unduly disturbing the plants.

HYDROHINT

Keeping a diary, no matter how rough, of hydroponic 'events', such as times of spraying, changing nutrient solution, special planting times, etc., will lead to more consistent yields. It also allows one to compare spectacular hydroponic results with the more pedestrian outcomes of traditional gardening.

Sweet peas growing in perlite.

Roses

Many perfect blooms develop on roses grown in buckets filled with perlite or granulated wool. Generally the quality is better than those grown in soil and the flowering period is longer. Commercial growers sing the praises of growool slabs for rose growing.

Silver Beet

Growool slabs seem to have been invented for the cultivation of silver beet. No problems have been experienced, provided the outer leaves are regularly harvested to eat.

Strawberries

A vertical black plastic sausage filled with perlite proved the most effective way to grow strawberries and Red Gauntlet the best all-round stock. Horizontal trays or tubes have been disappointing. To date the best strawberries have not been grown in the igloo but in a well sheltered glasshouse with screening against insects.

Strawflowers (Helichrysum)

Prolific harvests of these everlastings have been made from plants growing in granulated growool in household guttering. They needed no additional support even though they grow about 1 metre (3 ft 3 in) high.

Sweet Peas and Sweet William

These have produced excellent displays in either perlite or growool.

Tomatoes

Hydroponics suits tomatoes in a heart-warming fashion. The time and effort spent in establishing the system is fully justified by the enthusiasm shown by tomato plants to produce an excellent harvest. Grosse Lisse was the major type selected and generally did better in plastic buckets filled with granulated growool rather than perlite. Plants which were sown in midsummer would still be yielding perfect fruit early in winter. A key to success was the regular pruning as described in Chapter 6.

Tuberoses

These did not respond to the various conditions offered them and failed to flower.

Some hydroponic suppliers in Australia and New Zealand

In 1984 the Victorian Hydroponic Society published the results of a survey of hydroponic suppliers in Australia carried out by Dr Brian Hangar. A questionnaire was sent to thirty-five suppliers and twenty-five replies were received.

Over recent years the number of hydroponic suppliers has increased dramatically. Many have excellent displays and, by and large, the staff are enthusiastic and helpful to the beginner. Having done a number of surveys of suppliers, it is apparent that many of the smaller ones closed down or moved, but the overall increase in numbers continues.

The following pages list some of the known hydroponic outlets in Australia and New Zealand. A check in the Yellow Pages of your current telephone book may reveal other outlets not listed. It is suggested, as a general rule, and especially if some distance is involved, that you telephone suppliers before you visit them to determine the availability of what you desire to purchase. Another good source of information are gardening magazines and, in particular, the periodical *Practical Hydroponics and Greenhouses* (see Bibliography).

Along with the most up-to-date addresses and telephone/fax numbers we also indicate by a code what each supplies and any specialist supplies.

> **a** Caters for hobbyists
> **b** Supplies nutrients and media
> **c** Supplies hydroponic kits
> **d** Has hydroponic displays

Additional information when quoted is as received from the suppliers.

Suppliers who have not been listed are asked to write to Hyland House, 387-389 Clarendon Street, South Melbourne, Victoria 3205, for possible inclusion in a later printing.

Hydroponic Suppliers

ACT

AussieTrough
Unit 4, 19 Tennant St
Fyshwick 2609
Tel. (06) 239 1164
Fax (06) 239 1545
abc

New South Wales

Accent Hydroponics Pty Ltd
60 Bronte Rd
Bondi Junction 2026
Tel. (02) 369 4772
abcd
and
87–89 Marigold St
Revesby 2122
Tel. (02) 772 3166
abcd

Agri-Products
2/35 Lawson Cres.
Coffs Harbour 2450
Tel. (066) 51 6533
abcd
and
149 Prince St
Grafton 2460
Tel. (066) 43 2966
abcd

Aquaponics
(R and D Aquaponics)
13 Hallstrom Place
Wetherill Park   2164
Tel. (02) 756 1833
Fax (02) 756 2207
abcd

AussieTrough
12 Cawarra Rd
Caringbah 2229
Tel. (02) 525 0622
Fax (02) 525 4826
International:
Tel. + 61 2 525 0622
Fax + 61 2 525 4826
abc
and Newcastle shop:
9 Coorumbung Rd
Broadmeadow 2292
Tel. (049) 62 3255
Fax (049) 62 3202
abc

East Coast Hydroponics
12 Pittwater Rd
Manly 2095
Tel. (02) 9977 4116
Fax (02) 9977 4816
abcd
**Supplies a full range of horti-
cultural lighting systems.**

Fodder Factory (Aust) Pty Ltd
'Bobin Creek'
Via Wingham 2429
Tel./Fax (065) 50 5150
**Computer controlled environ-
ment growing systems.
Specialising in grass or fodder
growing with large units pro-
ducing up to one tonne of
green feed per day.**

Greenlight Hydroponics
252 Oxford St
Bondi Junction 2022
Tel. (02) 369 3928
Fax (02) 369 3961
abcd

Growool Horticultural Systems
Pty Ltd
(Mr Rick Donnan)
P.O. Box 120
Kurmond 2757
Tel. (045) 677 685
Fax (045) 677 684
**Wholesale supplier of horticul-
tural rockwool. Mr Donnan is
a hydroponic consultant.**

Hydroshop Corporation Pty Ltd
100 Darby St
Newcastle 2300
Tel. (049) 29 2370
Fax (049) 26 1377
abcd
and
Shop 2/390 The Esplanade
Warners Bay 2282
Tel. (049) 65 8131
abcd
and
Pacific Hwy
Raymond Terrace 2324 and
3 Chilcott Ave
Mount Hutton 2290
Tel./Fax (049) 65 7699
abcd

Indoor Sun Shop Australia
Pty Ltd
302 Hume Hwy
Liverpool 2170
Tel. (02) 822 4700
Fax (02) 822 5314
abcd
**Extensive range of horticultural
lighting.**

Lighting Components Pty Ltd
20 Barry Ave
Mortdale 2223
Tel. (02) 570 7322
Artificial lighting supplier.

Luwasa Hydroculture (Australia)
Ltd (wholesalers)
18 Rosebery Rd
Kellyville 2153
Tel. (02) 629 2311
Fax (02) 629 2122
bc
Indoor plants.

Nutriflo Hydroponic Systems
Unit 19, 5 Daintree Place
West Gosford 2250
Tel. (043) 231 599
abcd

Port Pumps and Irrigation
31 Jindalee Rd
Pt Macquarie 2444
Tel. (065) 81 1272
abcd

Simple Grow
(Homeplant Pty Ltd)
Corner Hassall and Widemere
Sts
Wetherill Park 2164
Tel. (02) 604 0469
Fax (02) 757 2774
abcd
and
Simple Grow
724 A Parramatta Rd
Croydon NSW 2132
abcd
**They state they are Australia's
biggest hydroponic factory.
Supplies delivered anywhere in
Australia or overseas.**

Soluble Solution Hydroponic Centres
525 Military Rd
Mosman 2088
Tel. (02) 968 2808
Fax (02) 968 2781
and
Head office/showroom:
31 Whiting St
Artamon 2064
Tel. (02) 439 5822
Fax (02) 439 8324
and
140 King St
Newtown 2042
Tel. (02) 565 1556
abcd

Water Well Irrigation
153 Industrial Rd
Oak Flats 2529
Tel. (042) 57 7500
Fax (042) 56 5839
abcd

Queensland

Accent Hydroponics
2086 Gold Coast Hwy
Miami 4220
Tel. (07) 5578 6111
Fax (07) 5578 6072
abcd

Addy Horticultural Supplies
374 North Deep Creek Rd
Gympie 4570
Tel. (074) 82 7730
abcd
Gives special advice and guidance for beginners. Facilitates hobbyists to become more commercially-oriented if required. Tailor-makes nutrient and hardware requests.

Allplas Extrusions Pty Ltd
9 Horizon Drive
(P.O. Box 1325)
Beenleigh 4207
Tel. (07) 287 2022
Fax (07) 807 3663
Supplies commercial and domestic hydroponic troughs and assorted hardware.

AussieTrough
Unit 4/56, Colebard St East
Archerfield 4106
Tel. (07) 3274 1020
Fax (07) 3274 2775
abc

Barmac Industries Pty Ltd
14 Annie St
Rocklea 4106
Tel. (07) 3277 3332
ab

E.T. Grow Home (Electric Terrarium)
4/13 Hicks St
(P.O. Box 1201)
Southport 4215
Tel. (075) 5591 6501
Fax (075) 5591 5119
abcd
Australian distributor for Milwaukee pH and E.C. meters.

Garden Friendly Products
Shop 3/1 Forest Ave
Kirwan 4817
Tel. (077) 73 7366
Fax (077) 73 7011
abcd

a	Caters for hobbyists
b	Supplies nutrients and media
c	Supplies hydroponic kits
d	Has hydroponic displays

The Hydroponic Warehouse
73 Pickering St
Enoggera 4051
Tel. (07) 3354 1588
Fax (07) 3354 3622
abcd
Supplies R and D nutrients, lights and grow chambers. Comprehensive displays well worth visiting.

Nerang Hydroponics
5/42 Lawrence Drive
Nerang 4211
Tel. (07) 5596 2250
abcd
Extensive range of indoor/outdoor equipment, including growlights.

Soluble Solution Hydroponic Centres
691 Ann St
Fortitude Valley 4006
Tel. (07) 252 5586
Fax (07) 852 1174
abcd

Sunstate Hydroponics
1137 Ipswich Rd
Moorooka 4501
Tel./Fax (07) 848 5288
and
67 Aerodrome Rd
Maroochydore 4558
Tel. (074) 791 011
abcd
Has agricultural scientist on staff for consultation.

South Australia

AussieTrough
Unit 4/12 Carsten Rd
Gepps Cross 5094
Tel. (08) 260 3333
Fax (08) 349 7755
abc

Greener Than Green
Cliff Avenue Garden Centre
52–54 Cliff Ave
Port Noarlunga South 5167
Tel. (08) 386 2596
abcd

Hydrocorp Pty Ltd
40 Pope St
Beverley 5009
Tel. (08) 244 4223
Fax (08) 347 2559
abcd
**Specialising in O.E.T.C.
systems which are an integrated form of the open end
systems as used in the UK and
The Netherlands.**

Hydroponic Hardware
12 Cavendish St
West Beach 5024
(GPO Box 812
Adelaide 5001)
Tel. (08) 356 3652
Fax (08) 235 0744
ac
**Specialises in manufacturing
and supplying NFT kits.**

Hydroponic Sales and Service
1 Salisbury Cres.
Colonel Light Gardens 5041
Tel. (08) 272 2000
abcd
**Commercial consultant
available.**

Magill Hydroponics
7 Ballantyne St
Magill 5072
Tel. (08) 364 4543
Fax (08) 332 0211
abcd

Pirie Plant Nursery
3 Copinger Rd
Port Pirie 5540
Tel. (086) 32 5299
ab

Solarome Hydroponics
44 Chapel St
Norwood 5067
Tel. (08) 362 8042
Fax (08) 363 0503
abcd
**Designs and builds systems for
clients.**

Tasmania

Hydroponic World
322 Bass Hwy
Sulphur Creek 7316
Tel. (004) 35 4411
Fax (004) 354 153
abcd

Island Hydroponics
26 Mulgrave St
Launceston 7250
Tel./Fax (004) 44 5588
abcd
**Also caters for commercial
growers.**

One Stop Grow Shop
213b Invermay Rd
Launceston 7250
Tel. (004) 26 7204
abcd

Tas Tech Hydroponics
206 Liverpool St
Hobart 7000
(002) 34 7824
abcd
Other store:
Shop 3 Brownell Place
11 Wilson St
Burnie 7320
abcd
Supplier of commercial equipment.

a	Caters for hobbyists
b	Supplies nutrients and media
c	Supplies hydroponic kits
d	Has hydroponic displays

Thorleys Garden Centre
55 Burnett St
New Norfolk 7140
Tel. (002) 61 3269
Fax (002) 61 3269
abcd

Victoria

Agromatic Corporation
Factory 12
176 Canterbury Rd
Bayswater 3153
Tel. (03) 9720 8288
Fax (03) 9720 8213
abcd
**Manufacturers of Auto-pot
systems**

AussieTrough
71 Shearson Cres.
Mentone 3194
Tel. (03) 9584 5622
Fax (03) 9583 7789
c
**Manufacturers of troughs and
kits.**

Australian Hydroponics
Silver St
Collingwood 3066
Tel. (03) 9416 1699
Fax (03) 9419 9755
abcd

Banksia Greenhouse and
Outdoor Centre
530 Burwood Hwy
Wantirna South 3152
Tel. (03) 9801 8070
Fax (03) 9887 3181
abcd

CV Hydroponics Bendigo
Shop 3/5 Wills St
Bendigo 3550
Tel. (054) 41 4866
abcd

Duralite Horticulture Supplies
54 Old Dandenong Rd
Heatherton 3202
Tel. (03) 9551 6756
Fax (03) 9558 0382
abcd

Echuca Hydroponic Nursery
23 Ogilvie Ave
Echuca 3564
Tel. (054) 80 2036
abcd

Ezy Gro
4 Station Rd
Rosanna 3084
Tel. (03) 9458 3233
abcd

The Fusco Plant Food Co.
P. O. Box 234
Bulleen 3105
Tel. (03) 9846 3401
Fax (03) 9846 3539
ab

Gardensmart
Shop 28 Gardenworld
810–834 Springvale Rd
Keysborough 3173
Tel./Fax (03) 9769 1411
abcd
Extensive range of Auto-pot systems and specialist kits, lighting, hot and shadehouses, and accessories.

Green Leaf Hydroponics
30 Walker Street
Dandenong 3175
Tel. (03) 9769 2418
Fax (03) 9794 0221
abcd
and
32/101–155 Beresford Rd
Lilydale 3140
Tel. (03) 9739 7311
Fax (03) 9739 7355
abcd

Greenlite Hydroponics
66b Chapel St
Windsor 3181
Tel. (03) 9510 6832
abcd
and
39 Burwood Hwy
Burwood 3125
Tel. (03) 9888 8885
Fax (03) 9888 8327
abcd
and
291 Mooroondah Hwy
Ringwood 3134
Tel. (03) 9870 1144
Fax (03) 9870 8566
abcd

Gro-Lite Australia (see 'Victorian Hydroponics' for retail outlets)
Factory 7/1 Austarc Ave
Thomastown 3074
Tel. (03) 9464 3980
Fax (03) 9464 3979
abcd
Gro-Lite Australia manufacture horticultural lighting equipment and are wholesalers of an extensive range of hydroponic supplies.

Grower's Choice Hydroponic Centre
Unit 1, 41–43 Allied Drive
Tullamarine 3043
Tel. (03) 9335 5394
Fax (03) 9335 2976
abcd
Specialises in supplying flood and drain (ebb and flo) tables.

Growtron
313 Glenhuntly Rd
Elsternwick 3185
Tel. (03) 9532 4228
Fax (03) 9532 7898
abcd

G V Hydroponics
Boundary Rd
Shepparton East 3631
Tel. (058) 29 2235
Fax (058) 29 2770
Mob. 018 597 188
abcd

Hanna Instruments Pty Ltd
18 Fiveways Blvd
Keysborough 3173
Tel. (03) 9769 0666
Fax (03) 9796 0699
a
Supplies instruments for testing pH, conductivity, temperature and humidity, with a helpful advisory and information service.

Hydroponic City
Cnr Dynon Rd and Radcliffe St
South Kensington 3031
Tel. (03) 9376 0447
Fax (03) 9376 0449
abcd

Hydroponic Distributor Supplies
Rohs Rd R.S.D.4
Bendigo East 3539
Tel. (054) 41 8284
Fax (054) 41 4164
b
Specialises in greenhouses.

Hydroponics World
Eliza Bottoms Nursery
27 Moorooduc Rd
Baxter 3911
Tel. (059) 71 1956
abcd
Supplier of pH and E.C. meters, pH increasers and pH decreasers.

Irelands Hydroponic and
Horticultural Lighting
10 Main St
Kinglake 3763
Tel. (057) 86 1280
Fax (057) 86 1286
abcd
Wholesale and commercial distributor servicing all Australian states. Australian distributor for Hydrofilm 'panda' black/white plastic film for hot house flooring and NFT channels. Free mail order catalogue.

Oasis Hydroponics
157 Tenth St
Mildura 3500
Tel. (050) 236 422
abcd

One Stop Sprinklers Pty Ltd
645 Burwood Hwy
Vermont South 3133
Tel. (03) 9800 2177
Fax (03) 9801 5751
abcd
Victorian distributor for Accent Hydroponics including 'panda' and 'jumbo' NFT channels; southern Australian distributor for NZ Hydroponics Ltd unique range of electronic control equipment.

Plastic Plumbing and Irrigation
Supplies
202 Pelham St
Carlton 3053
Tel. (03) 9347 6055
Fax (03) 9347 6006
Supplier of plastic fittings.

Sage Horticultural
121 Herald St
Cheltenham 3194
Tel. (03) 9553 3777
Fax (03) 9555 3013
abc

Up in Smoke
423 Sydney Rd
Brunswick 3056
Tel. (03) 9380 4689
abcd

Victorian Hydroponics
125 Spring St
Reservoir 3073
Tel. (03) 9478 6207
Fax (03) 9471 6207
abcd
and
39 McFarlane St
East Keilor 3033
Tel. (03) 9331 1600
Fax (03) 9331 1633
abcd
and
253 Princes Hwy
Dandenong 3175
Tel. (03) 9791 9900
Fax (03) 9791 9666
abcd
and
345 Lygon St
East Brunswick 3057
Tel. (03) 9380 6399
Fax (03) 9380 1877
abcd
and
Shop 1/104 Shannon Ave
Geelong West 3218
Tel. (052) 22 6730
Fax (052) 22 6930
abcd
Distributor of Gro-Lite Australia who manufacture horticultural lighting equipment.

Waterworks Horticultural Pty
Ltd
682a Warrigal Rd
Oakleigh South 3167
(P.O. Box 353
East Bentleigh 3165)
Tel. (03) 9570 3243
Fax (03) 9543 1684
abcd

Westend Hydroponics
Unit 30, 12–20 James Crt
Tottenham 3012
Tel. (03) 9315 2796
abcd

Western Australia

Aquaponics WA
Lot 12 Warton Rd
Canning Vale 6155
Tel. (09) 455 2133
Fax (09) 455 1818
abcd
Suppliers of all horticultural requisites including greenhouses, lighting, heating and cooling.

AussieTrough
56 King Edward Rd
Osborne Park 6017
Tel. (09) 244 1300
Fax (09) 445 3693
c

Flairform Products
3 Parkinson Lane
Kardinya 6163
Tel./Fax (09) 314 7595
abcd
Analytical chemists available for consultation, customised formulations prepared.

a Caters for hobbyists
b Supplies nutrients and media
c Supplies hydroponic kits
d Has hydroponic displays

Greenlite Hydroponics
662 Stirling Hwy
Mosman Park 6012
Tel. (09) 383 4933
abcd

Growth Technology
244 South Terrace
South Fremantle 6162
Tel. (09) 430 4713
Fax (09) 430 6939
abcd
**Manufactures hydroponic
nutrients. An excellent source
of advice and information.**

Guscottes
94–96 Marine Terrace
Geraldton 6530
Tel. (099) 21 2098
Fax (099) 64 1098
abcd
and
Harmar Sales and Hire
34 Chapman Rd
Geraldton 6530
Tel. (099) 21 2999
Fax (099) 21 8066
abcd

Hydroponic and Horticultural
Holdings
602 Albany Hwy
Victoria Park 6100
Tel. (09) 361 8211
Fax (09) 470 2036
abcd
**Manufactures equipment
including grow chambers,
flood/drain tables and NFT
systems.**

Hydroponic World
2 Seddon St
Subiaco 6008
Tel. (09) 388 3675
Fax (09) 384 5961
abcd
Lighting specialist.

Isabella's Hydroponic Nursery
and Garden Centre
66 Jambanis Rd
Wanneroo 6065
Tel./Fax (09) 306 3028
abcd

Moore - Better Gardens and Co.
4 Rockingham Rd
Sth Fremantle 6160
Tel. (09) 355 5524
Fax (09) 355 1102
bc

The Watershed Irrigation
Centre
1/146 Great Eastern Hwy
Midland 6058
Tel. (09) 274 3232
Fax (09) 274 3280
abcd
and
2874 Albany Hwy
Kelmscott 6111
Tel. (09) 495 1495
Fax (09) 390 5831
abcd
**Specialising in artificial lighting
equipment.**

New Zealand

Auckland Hydroponic Centre
Ltd
3 St Jude St
Avondale
Auckland NZ
Tel./Fax (09) 828 2352
abcd
**Supplier of NFT benches,
static gardens, monitoring
equipment and greenhouses,
pumps, books and magazines.**

Chartwell Hydroponics
53 Chartwell Ave
Glenfield
Auckland NZ
Tel./Fax (09) 444 5856
Mob. 025 822 952
abcd
**Catalogues available for pur-
chase. Supplies schools and
commercial growers.**

Down to Earth Garden Centre
164 Tahunanui Drive
Nelson NZ
Tel. (03) 548 5464
Fax (03) 548 5012
b

Evergreen Horticulture and
Hydroponics
14 Alloy St (P.O. Box 11 144)
Christchurch NZ
Tel. (03) 343 0190
Fax (03) 348 2110
abcd
**Suppliers of hydroponic mater-
ial and equipment for both
home and commercial growers
throughout the South Island.**

New Zealand Hydroponics Ltd
65 Chapel St
Tauranga NZ
Tel. (07) 578 0849
Fax (07) 578 0847
abcd
**Best known for its electronic prod-
ucts which are sold world-wide.
Products now well established in
world markets are the 'Dosetronic
L' hydroponic monitor controller,
the portable conductivity salts
meters variously named around
the world as 'The CF Truncheon',
'Quickdip nutrient meter' and
'Dipstick nutrient meter' as well
as the revolutionary auto calibrat-
ing (buffering) 'pH wand'.**

Northern Hydroponic Supplies Ltd
1/14 Agency Lane
(P.O. Box 163)
Silverdale NZ
Tel./Fax (09) 426 0295
abcd
**Both in and outdoor displays.
Installs and designs commercial
systems.**

Otaki Hydroponics Supplies Ltd
State Highway South
Otaki NZ
Tel. (06) 364 6243
Fax (06) 364 7206
Mob. 025 838 568
abcd
**Nutrient manufacturers to
'tailor-made' formulas.**

Phoenix 455 Greenworld
445 Ferguson St
Palmerston North NZ
Tel. (06) 358 5385
Fax (06) 358 5381
abc

---

a Caters for hobbyists
b Supplies nutrients and media
c Supplies hydroponic kits
d Has hydroponic displays

Suppliers of Seeds

There are plenty of sources of
seeds but some suppliers regularly introduce new or unusual
types and also produce catalogues filled with good advice.

Two such suppliers are:

New Gippsland Seed and Bulb
Company
P.O. Box 1
Silvan 3795
Tel. (03) 9737 9560
Fax (03) 9737 9292

Thompson and Morgan
Distributors: Eric Vale Australia
Pty Ltd
P.O. Box 50
Jannali 2226
Tel. (02) 533 3693

These two firms mail literature
and order forms upon request. If
writing, you should perhaps
enclose a stamp for return
postage.

Supplier of Carnation Plants

F. and I. Baguley
Flower and Plant Growers
Heatherton Rd
Clayton South 3169
Tel. (03) 9551 1266
Fax (03) 9551 7249

Supplier of Greenhouse Covers and Shadecloth Fabricators

Geoff Miller Pty Ltd
10–12 George St
Sandringham 3191
Tel (03) 9597 0777
Fax (03) 9598 1638

Supplier of Ludvig Svensson Screens

Commercial Glasshouses
39 Barry Rd
Kellyville 2153
Tel. (02) 629 2555
Fax (02) 629 2599

Supplier of Plastic Fittings

Plastic Plumbing and Irrigation
Supplies
202 Pelham St
Carlton 3053
Tel. (03) 9347 6055
Fax (03) 9347 6922
(Other Victorian outlets in
Geelong and Shepparton.)

Part-time Courses in Hydroponics

From time to time courses in hydroponics are run in various states by TAFE colleges or the Council for Adult Education. Special courses are occasionally advertised in *Practical Hydroponics and Greenhouses*. The following are the only courses which are known to be regularly available.

Australian Horticultural Correspondence School
P.O. Box 2092
Nerang East 4211
Tel (075) 304 855
and
264 Swansea Rd
Lilydale 3140
Tel. (03) 9726 9833
Mr John Mason coordinates an in-depth correspondence course which requires some 120 to 150 hours of study. This school also occasionally runs shorter courses.

College of Advanced Education
Wagga Wagga 2650
Mr A.C. Sunstrom runs an introductory course on hydroponics at the Riverina TAFE. His notes are used by a number of other TAFE colleges in Australia.

Holmsglen College of TAFE
Batesford Rd
Chadstone 3148
Tel. (03) 9567 1555
The short courses originally conducted by Mr Fred Funnell continue on a regular basis. They have proven very popular and are usually quickly booked out.

Kurri Kurri TAFE
The Kurri Kurri campus of the Hunter Institute of Technology has a semester course entitled 'Hydroponic Production' run by Ms Penny Dunstan, M.Ag. (Crop Science) Sydney.
For further information contact:
Rural Section
Kurri Kurri TAFE
Heddon St
(P.O. Box 135)
Kurri Kurri 2327
Tel. (049) 360 300
Fax (049) 360 360
email:
Penny.Dunstan@telsa.hl.com.au

Hydroponic Societies

The office bearers of hydroponic societies change over time. An up to date list of contact names and telephone numbers along with meeting dates is published regularly in *Practical Hydroponics and Greenhouses*.

Australia

Australian Hydroponic Association Inc.
Mr Bruce Retallick, Administrator
12 Jikara Drive
Glen Osmond 5064
Tel. (08) 379 1306
Fax (08) 338 2966
Mob. 014 099 848

New Zealand

Hydroponic Growers Association of New Zealand
P.O. Box 20-002
Te Rapa, Hamilton
New Zealand
Tel. (07) 856756

Singapore

Singapore Society for Soilless Culture
internet:
http://www.np.ac.sg:9080/~csk/hydro-html

USA

Hydroponic Society of America
2819 Crow Canyon Rd
Suite 218
San Ramon, CA 94583
Tel. (510) 743 9605
Fax (510) 743 9302
email: hydrosocam@aol.com
internet: http://www.intercom.
net/user/aquaedu/hsa/index.html

International society for soilless
culture (ISOSC)
People who become very serious
about hydroponics usually join
this Society, which provides the
very latest information and runs
international meetings, etc. The
offical representative of the
ISOSC for Australia, New
Zealand and the Pacific is:
Keith Maxwell, MSc
30 Sophia Cres.
North Rocks 2151
Mr Marshall says he will
welcome any enquiries.

Hydroponic Consultants

Information about consultants
can be obtained from State
Government Agricultural
departments. One held in particular high regard is Mr Rick
Donnan (see Growool
Horticultural Systems, Pty Ltd
in NSW, above).

Anyone even remotely con-
templating a commercial hydroponic venture should seek out a
consultant.

Bibliography

To keep up to date with the latest news and equipment, etc., on hydroponics, it is strongly recommended the reader subscribes to *Practical Hydroponics and Greenhouses*. Subscription details are available from Casper Publications Pty Ltd, P.O. Box 225, Narrabeen, NSW 2101. Telephone: (02) 9905 9933, Fax: (02) 9905 9030, email: casper@hydroponics.com.au, internet: http://www.world.net//hydroponics

Roger Fox, the editor of this magazine, which commenced publication in November 1991, manages to cater well for the home amateur as well as the professional commercial hydroponicer.

Carruthers, S. *Hydroponic Gardening*. Lothian, Melbourne. 1993.

Chapman, B., Penman, D. and Hicks, P. *The Garden Pest Book*. Nelson, Melbourne.1985.

Cheers, G. *Carnivorous Plants*. Carnivor and insectivor plants. P.O. Box 78, Diamond Creek, Victoria.1983.

Dalton, L. and Smith, R. *Hydroponic Gardening: A practical guide to growing plants without soil*. New Zealand Hydroponics Ltd, Tauranga, New Zealand.1993.

de Vaus, P. *Vegetables for Small Gardens and Containers in Australia*. Hyland House, Melbourne.1988.

Douglas, J.S. *Advanced Guide to Hydroponics*. Pelham Books, London. 1979.

French, J. *Natural Control of Garden Pests*. Aird Books, Melbourne. 1993.

Harris, D. *Hydroponics — The Complete Guide to Gardening without Soil*. Holland Press Ltd, London, UK. 1988.

Jones, L. *Home Hydroponics . . . and How To Do It*. Ward Ritchie Press, Pasadena, California, USA. 1977.

Mason, J. *Guide to Pests and Diseases*. Angus and Robertson, Sydney. 1995.

McMaugh, J. *What Garden Pest or Disease is That?* Lansdowne Publishing, Sydney. 1994.

Nicholls, R.E. (The Plant Doctor), *Beginning Hydroponics — Soilless Gardening: The Beginner's Guide to Growing Vegetables, House Plants, Flowers and Herbs Without Soil*. Running Press, Philadelphia, USA. 1994.

Parv, V. *Hydroponic Gardening*. Summit Books, Sydney. 1980.

Resh, H.M. *Hydroponic Home Food Gardens*. Woodbridge Press Publishing Company, Santa Barbara, California, USA. 1990.

Romer, J. *Hydroponic Gardening in Australia*. Reed, Sydney. 1986.

Rotter, H-A. *Growing Plants Without Soil*. E.P. Publishing Ltd, Germany. 1982.

Schubert, M. and Blaicher, W. *The ABC's of Hydroponics*. Sterling Publishing Company, New York, USA. 1984.

State Schools' Nursery. *School Hydroponics*. Published by State Schools' Nursery, Arthur Street, Oakleigh, Victoria. 1984.

Sundstrom, A.C. *Simple Hydroponics for Australian Home Gardeners*. Nelson. 1982.

Van Patten, G.F. *Gardening Indoors*. Van Patten Publishing, Portland, Oregon, USA. 1995.

Index

Numbers in bold type refer to major entries.